T0316522

Cambridge Elements ≡

Elements in Critical Heritage Studies
edited by
Kristian Kristiansen, *University of Gothenburg*
Michael Rowlands, *UCL*
Francis Nyamnjoh, *University of Cape Town*
Astrid Swenson, *Bath University*
Shu-Li Wang, *Academia Sinica*
Ola Wetterberg, *University of Gothenburg*

HERITAGE JUSTICE

Charlotte Joy
Goldsmiths, University of London

CAMBRIDGE
UNIVERSITY PRESS

CAMBRIDGE
UNIVERSITY PRESS

University Printing House, Cambridge CB2 8BS, United Kingdom

One Liberty Plaza, 20th Floor, New York, NY 10006, USA

477 Williamstown Road, Port Melbourne, VIC 3207, Australia

314–321, 3rd Floor, Plot 3, Splendor Forum, Jasola District Centre, New Delhi – 110025, India

79 Anson Road, #06–04/06, Singapore 079906

Cambridge University Press is part of the University of Cambridge.

It furthers the University's mission by disseminating knowledge in the pursuit of education, learning, and research at the highest international levels of excellence.

www.cambridge.org
Information on this title: www.cambridge.org/9781108820523
DOI: 10.1017/9781108900669

First published 2020

A catalogue record for this publication is available from the British Library.

ISBN 978-1-108-82052-3 Paperback
ISSN 2632–7074 (online)
ISSN 2632–7066 (print)

Heritage Justice

Elements in Critical Heritage Studies

DOI: 10.1017/9781108900669
First published online: October 2020

Charlotte Joy
Goldsmiths, University of London
Author for correspondence: joycharlotte@gmail.com

Abstract : *Heritage Justice* explores how far past wrongs can be remedied through compensatory mechanisms involving material culture. The Element goes beyond a critique of global heritage brokers such as UNESCO, the ICC and museums as redundant, Eurocentric and elitist to explore why these institutions have become the focus for debates about global heritage justice. Three broad modes of compensatory mechanisms are identified: recognition, economic reparation and return. Arguing against the view that museums should not be the site for difficult conversations about the past, *Heritage Justice* proposes that it is exactly the space around objects and sites created by museums and global institutions that allows for conversations about future dignity. The challenge for cultural practitioners is to broaden out ideas of material identity beyond source communities, private property and economic value to encompass dynamic global shifts in mobility and connectivity.

Keywords: anthropology, museum, International Criminal Court, repatriation, Benin Bronzes

ISBNs: 9781108820523 (PB), 9781108900669 (OC)
ISSNs: 2632–7074 (online), 2632–7066 (print)

Contents

Introduction

From the International Criminal Court (ICC) to European museums, debates about the ownership, protection and destruction of cultural heritage are increasingly making reference to notions of global justice in conjunction with object/site biographies. Beyond a legal framing of justice, an appeal is made to moral justice and to reparations for past wrongs in the present (Sørenson & Viejo-Rose, 2015). While a robust cosmopolitan defence (Cuno, 2009; Jenkins, 2018) has sought to relocate the argument both in the past and beyond the museum's walls, the same cosmopolitan logic invoked by the ICC brings it back to the present and questions Western museums' ethical stance on retention of colonial collections.

This Element will explore what is meant by the term 'justice' when applied to cultural heritage through the lens of two West African case studies. First, the case of the Benin Bronzes will be explored in relation to demands for return from Western museums (of objects, ownership and interpretation); second, the relation between international law and violent destructions of global heritage will be examined through the trial of the Malian Islamic extremist, member of Ansar Edine, Ahmad Al-Faqi Al-Mahdi at the ICC.

The Element will argue that a new 'heritage logic' is emerging which challenges a focus on the protection of cultural heritage for future generations premised on a post-war UNESCO model of the protection of global patrimony. A turn towards notions of justice, mirrored by political debates about intergenerational responsibility in economics (Pikkety, 2015) and the environment (Gore, 2006) together with the rise of populism and nationalism in the West has cast heritage practitioners into a new and complex role – that of arbitrators of global justice.

Heritage Justice explores how far past wrongs can be remedied through compensatory mechanisms involving material culture and questions whether past atrocities are in fact the targets of these compensatory claims. It will argue that the reckoning/compensation process is happening at an angle to the negotiation of the thing in itself. It is both real and a metaphor, at once material and transcendental.

It would be misleading to limit calls for return of objects or financial compensation for destruction of protected sites to the realm of discrete events, they are part of a vast flow of identity claims, moored and unmoored to specific objects and sites over time and place. The specific claims for return, financial compensation, or in relation to statues of colonial officials, destruction of material forms, can be theorised as interruptions in a global conversation about identity. These interruptions are about the way past atrocities are being felt in the present through global structural inequalities and discrimination.

There are two main reasons why museums and international heritage organisations are the current focus of these debates: first, they are institutions that make claims to global justice and thus provide their own internalised standard by which they are prepared to be judged; second, although the claims in themselves are vast, they can be contained and distilled into the reckoning over an object or site. This combination of worthy institution and manageable form means that cultural heritage has become a unique mechanism by which past atrocities can be reckoned with in the present.

Three broad modes of compensatory mechanisms are identified: recognition, economic reparation, and return. Arguing against Jenkins (2018) that museums should not be the site for difficult conversations about the past, *Heritage Justice* proposes that it is exactly the space around objects and sites created by museums and global institutions that allows for conversations about future dignity. The challenge for cultural practitioners is to broaden ideas of material identity beyond source communities, private property and economic value to encompass dynamic global shifts in mobility and connectivity.

The Conditions of Justice

In January 2002, I was looking through the window of a French bakery at their display of *Galettes des Rois* (epiphany cakes). On that particular year, the expensive bakery *Le Nôtre* had chosen a special theme for their '*fèves*' (the little porcelain beans that you find inside the cake – find the bean, become the King/Queen for the day) – the theme was 'African Masks' and seven different miniature approximations had been designed for the occasion (including one with visible scarification). It seemed to me a particularly unsettling form of cultural appropriation – African masks in Christian epiphany cakes, being eaten by well-heeled French consumers.

At the time, I was doing a masters dissertation looking at the politics of African material culture in Western museums. I had come to the conclusion that the economic value of the object in the museum was in many ways proportional to the harm felt by the community from whom the object had been taken (through the anthropological concept of authenticity via the art market). This same value was being invoked by Western museums as the reason why the objects could not be returned to Africa.

While in 2002 the African Mask *fèves* provoked no discernible public reaction, in 2019 discussions around cultural appropriation have intensified. The violation of other peoples' culture now seems more readily identified by the media – for example when festivalgoers apologise for wearing Native American headdresses, or fashion designers apologise for their use of sacred symbols during Paris Fashion Week.[1] In these cases, a negative emotional reaction on behalf of people invested in symbols and objects causes a retreat on behalf of those who have appropriated them.

A further condition needs to be present for the notion of justice to be invoked – the claim has to be considered legitimate by a critical mass of participants or potential consumers/citizens for the moral obligation to desist to have effect. Under these conditions, cultural appropriation is recognised as an illegitimate use or erasure of someone else's identity, whether or not it is for explicit political or economic reasons. The use has to be visible and through this visibility comes accountability.

If cultural appropriation/hybridity has been a constant throughout history, this Element seeks to identify how and when this flow is interrupted and under what conditions notions of justice are evoked and certain forms of appropriation rendered morally unconscionable. Although repatriation claims have been present for as long as museums have held objects considered by others to belong to them, the recent acceleration in number and profile of claims has caught many museum professionals off guard. The presence of colonial collections in Western museums has shifted uncomfortably into the justice sphere and para-doxically, the more visible and receptive museums are being in response to claims for access, the louder the cry for justice through return becomes.

A State's Aladdin's Cave?

'Justice As Return' will take up this theme and explore the conditions under which repatriation claims begin to matter to a critical mass of people on a global stage. The case of the Benin Bronzes, looted by the British in 1897, has mattered a great deal ever since to the Oba of Benin and his people. In 2002, during a debate in the UK House of Commons, Tim Loughton MP spoke of the Benin Bronzes in relation to a tabled debate around the fate of the Parthenon Friezes/ Elgin Marbles:

> Decontextualisation would be a disaster and would open a Pandora's box, whatever the hon. Member for Knowsley, South says. Mesopotamian finds dug up because of the tenacity of British archaeologists in the 1900s and previously would be returned to Iraq and Iran, perhaps never to be seen again. The Benin bronzes would go to Nigeria, despite the fact that the British museum helped to build the collection of bronzes in Nigeria itself and has done an awful lot to promote the heritage and history of west Africa. When Nelson Mandela visited the British museum just 13 months ago on the opening of three new African galleries, he praised the British museum as:

---

[1] Cf. Zuhair Murad *Indian Summer* Spring 2018 Couture Collection.

'this truly international institution for enriching and cross-fertilising the world's institutions'.[2]

Usefully for the purpose of this Element, Tim Loughton MP, continued:

> What are the real motives? It is all political. Academically, there is no case to return the Elgin marbles and other works of art to Athens. They are in the ownership of the British Museum but they belong to the history of world civilisation. To treat them as some political trophy that can be traded for short-term political advantage is the worst reason for ripping them out of the heart of one of the world's great museums. The British museum should not be treated as *some state Aladdin's cave* to buy power and influence at random. (my emphasis)

Since that debate, museums across the world have changed their position and in 2018 the Benin Dialogue Group[3] (comprising of representatives from museums with the most important Benin collections, representatives of the Oba of Benin and the Nigerian Government) have agreed to build a museum in Benin City to house a permanent 'loaned' collection of bronzes. 'Justice As Return' will chart the journey from the arrogant political indifference of 2002 to today's desperate attempts by museums to maintain a moral link with collections that many now regard as never having belonged to them at all.

Justice and Destruction

The call for destruction of statues, such as the 'Rhodes Must Fall' movement that began in 2015, whilst also making claims to social justice through materiality, is different from repatriation claims because the debate is over the representation of history through the glorification of individuals, not through the appropriation of someone else's heritage. Both movements for repatriation and destruction consider historical events and their consequences to be central to ongoing inequalities and societal divides, but only the repatriation claims posit a physical link between the object in the museum and the descendants of the object makers/users. The logic is that while the statue of Cecil Rhodes may fill me with rage as I walk past it, the object in the museum causes me grief in its absence; it is exiled and needs to be returned for healing to take place. Both the absence of objects and presence of statues cause physical distress that can be remedied through relocation or removal.

---

[2] *Hansard*, 5 Feb 2002: Column 778.

[3] The Benin Dialogue Group established a Steering Committee composed of representatives from European museums (Museum am Rothenbaum, Kulturen und Künste der Welt (MARKK); Ethnologisches Museum, Berlin; British Museum London; NWVW; The purpose is to distinguish between the three types of participants: the European museums, the Nigerian govt and the royal court of Benin NWVW is Dutch National Museum of World Cultures), the National Commission for Museums and Monuments, Nigeria, Edo State Government and the Royal Court of Benin.

While the mechanisms by which the presence and absence of objects in these two cases provoke distress are different, the historical periods both justice movements reference share the same roots of racism, brutal oppression and shame. Calls for repatriation or for Rhodes to fall are not limited to historical crimes but are the recognition of the ongoing discrimination and harm felt by many today. The argument goes that as both the apartheid regime in South Africa and colonialism are now recognised by the international community as crimes against humanity, how can heritage practitioners today justify the preservation of the material embodiment of these crimes in their museums and public spaces?

One answer may be in the resilience of the idea of the mythical apolitical museum space: a liminal utopia where only universal aesthetics and scientific learning count. The second may be a misplaced faith in the political power of the present, where 'the past is a foreign country, they do things differently there' (Lowenthal, 1985), when all along the insight has been that the present is saturated with the consequences of past injustices. The third may be the current unsettling nature of performative destructions of global cultural heritage by Islamic extremists and the way in which a disregard for the sanctity of human lives and attacks on the material manifestations of people's dignity have been calculatedly woven together to cause maximum harm. These present crimes against humanity are brought into intellectual proximity with past crimes and distinctions between the two are harder to uphold.

Macron's Pledge

Emmanuel Macron became the President of France in May 2017 with his new party 'La République en Marche' promising sweeping social and economic reforms. His relationship with sub-Saharan Africa emerged in the light of past failed attempts by French presidents to forge new relationships with former French colonies. These difficult relationships are probably best illustrated by a speech given by Nicolas Sarkozy (President of France from May 2007–May 2012) in Dakar, Senegal in 2007. In the speech, Sarkozy stated:

> I want to say to you, youth of Africa that the tragedy of Africa is not in the so-called inferiority of its art, its thought, its culture. Because, in what concerns art, thought and culture it is the West that learnt from Africa. Modern art owes almost all to Africa.

And then the infamous phrase:

> *The tragedy of Africa is that the African has not fully entered into history.* (my emphasis) The African peasant, who for thousands of years have lived

according to the seasons, whose life ideal was to be in harmony with nature, only knew the eternal renewal of time, rhythmed by the endless repetition of the same gestures and the same words ... This man (the traditional African) never launched himself towards the future. The idea never came to him to get out of this repetition and to invent his own destiny.

Sarkozy then goes on to list the many problems faced by 'Africa' such as nostalgia for a golden age that never was, a desire for a mythical past, a resignation to misfortune, not recognising that globalisation is a good thing and a general disengagement from the world.[4]

Even by the standards of the day, the speech was astonishingly racist and insulting and caused an immediate global media backlash. Yet the fact Sarkozy, the newly elected French president, felt able to say these things, to address a whole continent as one (this insult is listed by Felwine Sarr in his work '*Afrotopia*' (2016) as one of the many recurring racist tropes used by Western leaders) and to generalise in such lazy ways the 'failings' of a continent while only paying lip service to the brutal dehumanisation of slavery and colonialism, is testimony to the ongoing asymmetry of the relationship between France and its former colonies.

In contrast, and in order to create a rupture with Sarkozy's approach, Macron's speech at the University of Ouagadougou (Burkina Faso) in November 2018 starts far more humbly:

I was told that this auditorium was Marxist and pan-African. I therefore said to myself: 'This may be the place where I have to go to speak!' Because I did not come here to tell you that we were going to make a great speech to start a new chapter in France and Africa's relationship. Nor did I come to tell you what France's policy for Africa should be, as some people may claim. Because there no longer is a French policy for Africa![5]

He goes on to try and demonstrate that he is a new president with a different political postcolonial outlook:

I would never pretend to express the complexity and diversity of a continent made up of 54 countries. First because it would be terribly arrogant to attempt to explain that there is absolute unity and complete uniformity; 54 countries, each with its own history, with even more ethnicities and languages, with relationships that are not the same with regard to France and a past very often full of very different traumas.

---

4   www.dibussi.com/2007/09/in-his-own-word.html (accessed 29 July 2019) and full French text www.lemonde.fr/afrique/article/2007/11/09/le-discours-de-dakar_976786_3212.html.
5   www.elysee.fr/emmanuel-macron/2017/11/28/emmanuel-macrons-speech-at-the-university-of-ouagadougou.en.

Macron then goes on to explain that he is part of a new generation of Europeans, who live within the shadow of colonialism but were not directly implicated in it. He therefore wants to meet his audience as an equal, as part of a young generation of Europeans and Africans that need to work together to face global challenges. In a similar vein to his post Gilets Jaunes policy in France, he launches a vast 'listening exercise' where he commits to hear what is being said by young people across Africa.

Next, the link with the migration crisis is made and he pledges to work with African countries to try and stabilise the movement of people from Africa to Europe by planning a joint evacuation plan of migrants trapped in Libya:

> We cannot let hundreds of thousands of Africans who have no chance of obtaining asylum, some of whom may spend years in Libya, face all the dangers of the Mediterranean and run into this tragedy.

Once migration is acknowledged as a problem for both France and Africa, Macron sets out a number of measures to create the '450 million jobs that Africa will need by 2050'. These are infrastructure projects, training, digital campuses, loans for small and medium size companies, the support of women into the workplace and the movement of more young people from France to Africa and vice versa.

At the end of his speech, he addresses the lack of trust that many people in the audience in Ouagadougou must inevitably feel towards yet another French leader promising to transform their lives. Macron terms it as a 'loss of shared imagination' and proposes three solutions:

> The first remedy is culture. In this area, I cannot accept that a large share of several African countries' cultural heritage be kept in France. There are historical explanations for it, but there is no valid, lasting and unconditional justification. African heritage cannot solely exist in private collections and European museums. African heritage must be showcased in Paris but also in Dakar, Lagos and Cotonou; this will be one of my priorities. Within five years I want the conditions to exist for temporary or permanent returns of African heritage to Africa.

This part of the speech signalled a step change in cultural policy in France and led to the commissioning of a report on the subject by two academics, Felwine Sarr and Bénédicte Savoy published in 2018 as 'The Restitution of African Cultural Heritage: Towards a New Relational Ethics', known colloquially as the 'Macron Report' or the 'Sarr/Savoy Report'. The report was limited in its remit to objects from sub-Saharan Africa held in French museums but has had a great impact on discussions about restitution from European museums to Africa more broadly (discussed in 'Justice As Return').

Interestingly, Macron's other two solutions for a 'loss of shared imagination' are sport and the French language. In relation to sport, he offers African athletes the opportunity to train in France in anticipation of the 2024 Paris Summer Olympics. In relation to the French language, Macron urges young Africans to embrace French and make it their own through the ongoing project of the '*francophonie*'. He would like French to become the language of Africa, despite English being the current 'fashionable' choice and many African intellectuals calling for a return to the mother tongue.

During his presidential campaign in 2017, Emmanuel Macron was already rethinking France's relationship with its past by describing France's action in Algeria and its wider colonial project as a 'crime against humanity'. This sober reckoning provoked fierce criticism from right-wing politicians in France but was probably an astute positioning for Macron, who, at only thirty-nine years old when he was elected, was well placed to discern a generational shift in thinking about social justice.

Negotiations around heritage and justice can therefore be seen to be framed within a specific political and economic moment whilst being overshadowed by past (mostly failed) attempts at creating equal and respectful relationships between Europe and its former colonies. As Diagne (2011) reminds us in his *African Art as Philosophy: Senghor, Bergson and the Idea of Negritude*, African philosophy and art have historically been co-opted by European intellectuals to stand for something other: for example the existential impossibility of being known as yourself through the other's gaze (Sartre) or the fundamental impulse of art as knowledge (Picasso). What the return of African objects from European museums should allow for is a rupture with a constant return to the European self through thinking about 'the other'. However, what current events seem to be illustrating is that this is in fact not the case, the return of objects, like their acquisition in the first place, is bound up with trade, economic impulses, European cultural redemption and the ongoing asymmetry in global power and influence.

Justice As Return

Those versions of whiteness that produced men like Rhodes must be recalled and de-commissioned if we have to put history to rest, free ourselves from our own entrapment in white mythologies and open a future for all here and now. Mbembe[6]

The Landscape of Justice

Despite being aimed at museums and focusing on particular objects, repatriation claims rely on a grammar of justice that reference many broader debates and historical events. What may at first have been seen as a chaotic assemblage of grievances and events, both contemporary and historic, seems in time to have coalesced around a powerful emotional and political truth: that instead of leading to greater understanding and equality between cultures, museums with colonial era collections are systematically reproducing colonial era power relations in the present.

The task of the curator with colonial era collections has therefore become one of understanding the link that exists between historical and contemporary events. These include the Black Lives Matter movement, the Grenfell Tower disaster, and the Windrush scandal in the UK. Authors such as Jenkins (2018) and Cuno (2009) reject this challenge and take refuge in their view of the museum as an encyclopaedic and cosmopolitan space, operating outside of history and politics. This theoretical flight from responsibility has a long intellectual pedigree (cf. Arendt on responsibility). The problem with their position is that contemporary political events demonstrate that the 'version of whiteness' still alive and well today continues to lead to systematic racism, the same systematic racism that led colonial officials, explorers and military men to dispossess people from their cultural heritage during the colonial encounter.

This logic (of the museum's continual complicity in marginalisation and exclusion) has seen a growing number of parallel debates been brought in to the support the repatriation cause. For example, the British Petroleum (BP) funding of the British Museum has been brought together conceptually by activists with calls for the for the return of Hoa Hakananai'a, a sculpted basalt head removed from Rapa Nui in 1868. Here, the British Museum stands accused of putting financial gain before environmental responsibility in the same way as it disregards the lives of a community of people in the Pacific who would like to be reunited with one of their ancestors in exile. It is colonial era arrogance, alive and well in 2019. Once that first conceptual link is made, between powerful museum institution and powerless person(s), more links inevitably follow, most

---

[6] https://africaisacountry.atavist.com/decolonizing-knowledge-and-the-question-of-the-archive.

recently the Gilets Jaunes movement in France included repatriation of African objects from French museums in their new political manifesto[7].

The Logic of Restitution

In her important work on international law, museums and the return of cultural objects, Vrdolkaj (2006) identifies three main reasons for return. The first is a restoration of a 'sacred' link between people and objects, the second is a way of remedying wrongful acts (including genocide) and the third is fulfilling people's right to self-determination. In certain cases, the retained ownership of collections by museums is a way of retaining animosity between states or between the state and indigenous groups in what turns out to be an ongoing condition of harm and conflict (2006: 300).

Every time a museum announces to the media that it will part with objects in its collection, it is contributing towards a gradual but discernible shift in attitudes about the validity of repatriation claims. Throughout 2018 and 2019 there has been a steady flow of announcements: amongst many others, the Quai Branly museum's promise to return twenty-six thrones and statues taken in 1892 during a colonial war against the then Kingdom of Dahomey and Oslo's Kon-Tiki museum's return of object collected by Thor Heyerdahl to Chile. The claims tend to follow a familiar pattern:[8]

1. An object or assemblage of objects are identified by an external party (a state, descendants of the users or creators of the objects or a specific group of people for whom the object has unique cultural resonance) as being contested.
2. The party/parties requesting the return make a public and emotional case.
3. The museum defends the presence of the objects in their collection (perhaps linking it to some Western intellectual tradition or historical figure) yet acknowledges the potential validity of other claims.
4. The museum undertakes a period of research on the object(s) in order to frame their response.
5. Having 'scientifically' considered the claim, the museum returns the object-(s) in a ceremony that commands positive media coverage.

Over recent decades, museums have found this approach to repatriation increasingly hard to defend. The seemingly cold 'scientific' approach of the museum is at odds with the more immediate and emotionally compelling claims of those requesting the return of their heritage. At play here is the universal story of

---

[7] www.carmah.berlin/reflections/restitution-report_first-reactions/.
[8] This process does not hold for the many repatriation cases that take place behind the scenes – these would usually concern human remains that belong to a different ethical and legal category.

return to the homeland, a story that finds echoes in all cultures and has enormous symbolic and emotional resonance. It is hard to see how a museum could mount a convincing defence of a position of retention because objects are both human-like enough to be invested with human sentiment but object-like enough to be allowed to face uncertain material futures.

In the *Silence du Totem* (Ngom, 2018), a fictionalised idealised version of this universal story is told. Sitoé Le Goff is a young Senegalese anthropologist who leaves a happy childhood in Senegal to study and work in Paris. There she meets and falls in love with a Frenchman, has a child and gets her dream job at the Quai Branly Museum. Despite her devotion to her new life and career, she is unsettled by the presence of an African statue that is housed in a secret collection belonging to the museum. This secret collection is kept out of sight and occasionally objects from it are sold to an elite group of international collectors when the museum needs to raise money. Sitoé is asked to curate a private exhibition of the secret collection to be viewed by a Russian collector who will choose one object for purchase.

Gradually, she discovers that the statue that has so unsettled her came from her grandfather's village in Senegal and is in fact a totemic object 'La Statue de Pangool', the repository of her ancestors' souls. During her research, she tracks down the granddaughter of the missionary, the man who exploited the political tensions in the village to unfairly purchase the statue. By gaining her trust, she gets access to his diaries and thus has written evidence of what she has emotion-ally known all along: that the missionary knew that he was committing an unethical and illicit act (echoing Griaule and Leiris, discussed below). She confronts the director of the Quai Branly with her findings and despite seeming to listen and understand her position, he is implacable in the museum's position of no return. Sitoé then turns to officials at the United Nations Education Social and Cultural Organisation (UNESCO) and, with the support of the granddaughter of the missionary who took the statue, puts together a case for its return (including a journey with UNESCO officials back to the village in Senegal). Further urgency is given to her quest when her young son is struck down with a mystery illness that she suspects is linked to the absence of the statue from the village shrine. She finds out from her father that after the theft of the statue was discovered (a theft enabled by her great-uncle), a curse was pronounced on the descendants of the family that should have protected the shrine (her great-grandfather). The curse stated that all firstborn males of the lineage would die until the return of the statue to its rightful place. By convincing the UNESCO officials of the validity of her claim, she therefore not only returns her cultural heritage to its home but also saves her son's life (and by consequence herself/her own future).

Like traditional quest stories, *Le Silence du Totem* follows the pursuit for justice through a journey that turns out to have been set in motion many generations before. The fact that repatriation claims so convincingly fit this narrative and weave together individual redemption with a responsibility for the past and to our 'authentic' selves, (however alienated we have become through contemporary life) ensures that the media will continue to take an active interest in them. In contrast, the passions of the museum's curators are seen as outdated and contrived.

From Colonial Heroes to Contemporary Pariahs

After the claimant and the curator, the third pillar in the story of return is the collector, the person who brought the objects to the museum in the first place. Over time, the 'heroic' journeys of early missionaries, colonial officials and collectors have been rewritten as stories of dispossession and violence. In his account of the Dakar-Djibouti colonial expedition funded by the French State in the early 1930s, Michel Leiris recounts the numerous ways in which the people they encountered were tricked, robbed or violently disposed of their cultural heritage. In a diary entry on the 7 September 1931, Leiris records:

> Before leaving Dyabougou (central Mali), we visit the village and make off with a second *kono* (sacred object) which Griaule found by slipping surreptitiously into the special hut ... My heart is beating very loudly because, since yesterday's fiasco, I am more keenly aware of the enormity of our crime (2017: 156)

And later the same day, after taking yet another sacred object without consent, Leiris reflects:

> I realize in a dazed stupor, which only later transforms into disgust, that you feel pretty sure of yourself when you are a white man with a knife in your hand (2017: 156)

What place do these colonial narratives have in a contemporary museum display? The truth seems to be that they are given very limited visibility and rarely ever displayed in conjunction with the objects whose acquisition they describe. Instead, acquisition labels are discreet numeric plaques that convey order and bureaucracy, far removed from the human tragedies they are indexing. The British Museum's display of Benin Bronzes is hung alongside an explanatory panel entitled: 'The Discovery of Benin Art by the West' with the following explanation:

> In the 1890s Benin resisted British control over Southern Nigeria. In March 1897, retaliating for the killing of British representatives, a punitive expedition conquered the capital. Thousands of treasures were taken as booty, including around 1000 brass plaques from the palace.

In a continuing Eurocentric vein, the explanation continues: 'Benin treasures caused an enormous sensation, fuelling appreciation for African art which profoundly influenced 20th Century Western Art'. The panel continues by explaining that after the expedition the British Museum purchased the plaques together with about sixteen other museums mostly in Britain and Germany and that since the 1970s, when an interest in Benin Art increased, approximately eighty-five museums in eighteen countries now have their own collections of Benin Art.

By the use of words such as 'resistance', 'retaliation' and 'conquered' the British Museum is perpetuating a myth of ethical acceptability of British colonial actions. This same myth of acceptability is enthusiastically taken up by politicians, the latest in 2019 being the UK Conservative Culture Minister, Jeremy Wright, who announced that there would be no legislative change to allow for repatriation of colonial collections, citing the need for 'single point' destinations to see world art. For African philosophers such as Mbembe, this 'debt of truth' is a core responsibility for museums, one that most are careful to avoid.[9]

'Owning' Your Heritage (or Brutal Past)

Over the last few decades, European museums with Benin collections have faced increasing demands for the return of the looted treasures by the subsequent Obas of Benin and the Nigerian Government. The most recent claimant is Ewuare II (crowned in 2016) whose coronation had to take place without many of the royal ritual objects now dispersed around the world.

The Benin Dialogue Groups' (BDG) announcement that it will build a permanent museum in Benin City and 'lend' objects on a rotating basis to ensure a permanent display has been met with unsurprising dismay amongst much of the West African Press. Headlines such as 'Nigeria To Borrow Looted Nigerian Artefacts From Successors Of Looters: Neo-Colonialist Cultural Imperialism At Work'[10] sum up the mood of many who point out that there is little likelihood that Western museums would suggest a similar model to countries such as China. There is therefore something uniquely humiliating in the relationship between the West and Africa, and that humiliation is played out again and again by tone-deaf museum professionals in their concern for objects. In answer to criticism, the BDG have stressed that the creation of the new museum is not the end point of the negotiations and does not change the ongoing demands for permanent restitution of the Bronzes. However, as Savoy (the co-author of the Macron Report) has recently commented on the British Museum's position of non-return:

---

[9] www.lemonde.fr/festival/article/2019/08/13/achille-mbembe-l-afrique-laboratoire-vivant-ou
-s-esquissent-les-figures-du-monde-a-venir_5498991_4415198.html.

[10] www.africavenir.org.

> It's not us who are radical; it's historical facts which are radical. There was a taboo around this fact for many centuries in Europe, the fact that many major museums have collections based on plundering. There are always ruptures when you break a taboo.[11]

From assessing media coverage across Europe, there seems a clear shift in political discourse marked by the publication of the Macron report. Journalists are making space in their coverage for the claimant's voice to be heard, while the views of museum professionals lack emotional conviction and revert to bureaucratic and legal defences.

Putting aside the rhetorical battle going on between those on both sides of the repatriation debate, a major factor remains the wealth and power of the countries housing the colonial collections in comparison with the wealth and power of the countries asking for return. This economic gap and the power relations it allows are increasingly being seen as both a result and constitutive of ongoing inequalities. The return of colonial collections has become a matter of economic and social justice, not curatorial or art historical concern. In 'Decolonizing Knowledge and the Question of the Archive' Mbembe reflects on Fanon's insights:

> As a theory of self-ownership, decolonization is therefore relational, always a bundle of innate rights, capabilities and claims made against others, taken back from others and to be protected against others – once again, by force if necessary. In his eyes, self-ownership is a precondition, a necessary step towards the creation of new forms of life that could genuinely be characterized as fully human. (2015: 12)

It can therefore be argued that full and unconditional repatriation is the necessary precondition for meaningful decolonisation and 'new forms of life'. The rupture so feared by museums (rupture of knowledge, collections, materiality) could be seen as a positive side effect of repatriation, leaving newly reconfigured museums in the West to think about their identity and potential to become 'fully human' institutions and meaningfully address the interests and concerns of the communities they serve in 2019.

An 'Anti-racist' Factory?

In a debate on *Radio France International* in November 2018 on the subject of the restitution of African art, Julien Volper, a curator at the Royal Museum for Central Africa (Tervuren) describes the Quai Branly Museum in Paris as 'an

---

[11] Bakare, L. 'British Museum "has head in sand" over return of artefacts' *Guardian Newspaper* (21 June 2019) www.theguardian.com/culture/2019/jun/21/british-museum-head-in-sand-return -artefacts-colonial.

anti-racist factory' and claims that global museums have played a key role in showcasing African art to change the West's view of Africa.[12] He does not elaborate on the mechanism by which people's racist attitudes are changed by an appreciation of art, but one can suppose that, together with the British Museum, the West's 'discovery of African art' is somehow something that reflects well on global museums. As well as 'discovering' African art, valuing African art by including it in global museums may be what Volper has in mind.

However, by decontextualising the art and locating it not in a contemporary African present but in an imagined past, the Western ethnographic museum often has the effect of creating a distance between real lives and objects. For example, in Paris both people and objects are existing far from their homelands and it seems that the objects are valued, cared for and welcomed in a way that people, especially young undocumented male migrants from sub-Saharan Africa, are not. It does not seem that ethnographic objects visibly making their homes in Paris have made it any easier for people from whose communities they were taken to feel at home there too (Thomas, 2013). Objects taken during the colonial encounter do not seem to have created anticipatory 'archives of welcome' for the people who eventually followed. Instead, the ethnographic objects in the Quai Branly entered the reified world of the art market and were dispossessed of their quotidian human connections (apart from those that narrate the object's authenticity and economic value, usually through reference to ritual use).

Volper's optimistic reading of the Quai Branly can be juxtaposed with a detailed ethnography of the institution, Sally Price's *Paris Primitive* (2007). Her study charts the way in which the Quai Branly Museum was born out of the voracious appetites for African art of both the French president Jacques Chirac and his art dealer Jacques Kerchache. It does not paint a flattering picture of the personal motivations or the political machinations that led to the collections to come together in the Quai Branly, nor can any visitor of the museum not be struck by the exoticising architecture and troubling 'primitive' categorisation of the collections. In fact, it would not be difficult to describe the museum, with its high entrance price and decontextualised presentation of objects as art, as exacerbating the ongoing marginalisation of people from sub-Saharan Africa living in France today.

Additionally, the Quai Branly, like many ethnographic museums, has a close association with the art market (see figure 1). They are both

---

[12] www.rfi.fr/emission/20181125-restitution-oeuvres-art-afrique.

Figure 1 Promotional poster for the 'Picasso Primitif' exhibition held at the Quai Branly Museum in 2017

Credit: Photo © musée du quai Branly - Jacques Chirac, Dist. RMN-Grand Palais / image musée du quai Branly - Jacques
Chirac Photo © Herbert List / Magnum Photos © Succession Picasso 2017

driven by 'passions' for collecting and foreground the aesthetic over the ethnographic. This can be seen by the way in which the Quai Branly displays the works, with written contextualisation placed at a distance from the objects or provided as handouts so as not to distract from the visitor's aesthetic experience. This art historical reading of African art has the effect of shifting debates about return from matters of social justice to matters of universal aesthetics. Universality is also invoked to suggest that the objects occupy a different temporality, and are somehow operating out of time: they are in a liminal (quasi-religious) state and vulgar human demands for their return are dismissed as the political machinations of the moment, whimsical, short-sighted and in time to be regretted.

Furthermore, African art in Western museums is part of a universal art history in multiple ways: as art, as inspiration for non-African artists, as commentary on the 'other' during the colonial encounter, as self-commentary of the artist, as abstract, as economic repository, as ethnography and so on.

In a short novel *Des Lions Comme des Danseuses* written in 2015, Arno Bertina describes an imagined future relationship between Africa and Europe brought about by the consequences of thinking through the repatriation debate. In his story, the Quai Branly Museum is gradually convinced to grant free access to its collections for Bamilékés nationals (a people of Cameroon). The ease with which the museum surrenders to the demand alerts political leaders in Cameroon to the fragile nature of the hold Western museums have over their colonial collections: 'If the French had given so easily (to the demand for free entry), it was a sign that they had a lot more to lose in this story' (2015: 26, my translation). And what they have to lose is the collections themselves, which they are forced to present as part of a common humanity in order to maintain moral ownership. There follows a series of demands involving the free movement of African nationals to visit their patrimony in exile through the granting of free 'culture' visas, leading politicians all over Europe to despair: 'What humanitarian action had not achieved through family reunion policies, was going to be achieved by simian totems and mothed ornaments' (2015: 36, my translation). Then comes the next logical step: that Western art (so influenced as it has been by the non-Western art in European collections) should be lent to African museums. The great treasures of Europe therefore need to leave the continent (a prospect that makes two Western curators faint as they drink beers in the Grand-place in Brussels). The final step is the removal of all borders and the full free movement of people. In this imaginary tale, the free movement of people and objects in the name of cultural diplomacy stands in stark contrast to the control of borders and thousands of deaths in the Mediterranean in the name of migration policy.

When asked about his 2015 fable in the light of the Macron report in 2018, the author explained that he wrote the story after a trip to Cameroon where he had met the king of Bangoulap (a small kingdom in Cameroun) who had complained to him about the need to pay twelve euros to see his heritage in the Quai Branly Museum. Commissioned to write a book about European identity, Bertina decided to do so through the continent's rela-tionship with Africa:

Since the Schengen Agreement in 1985, Europe defines itself only in a military, closed fashion. When it came to writing about Europe, I was happy to take a side look and think about it in relation to Africa. To close yourself off from your neighbours is a symptom of a dying entity. In terms of paradoxical utopias – the Europe in this fable feels like it is falling apart when it is in fact re-building itself.[13] (my translation)

As commented on by Bénédicte Savoy (co-author of the Macron report) in a postscript to the book: the fate of objects removed in times of conflict have always been part and parcel of museum identities in relation to the particular political moment in which they find themselves. National museum collections were brought together for political purposes and narrate a particular version of history: the history of the conqueror, not the conquered. As relationships between countries change, pressure is put on museums to reflect that change in their display, granting of access and attitudes towards their collections. Since the display of colonial collections during world fairs and colonial exhibitions was instrumental in selling the (tax-payer funded) colonial trade project to the European masses (Morton, 2000), perhaps the return of the objects will be instrumental in future trade partnerships and public opinion will be bought on side to support this new economic strategy.

Circularity of Circulation

Whereas public opinion seems to have shifted towards an active and open interest in repatriation claims, not everyone has been enthusiastic about the Macron report and its potential consequences. After a seemingly open-minded first reaction, curators, museum directors, politicians and art historians have started to distance themselves from notions of return and instead gravitate towards the term 'circulation'. Like the most loved material culture concept of 'entanglement' (Thomas, 1991), the concept of circulation allows museum professionals to avoid the fixity of ownership, whilst retaining its advantages. In this vision, objects are constantly in flow and the period of colonialism was one of cultural exchange which although acknowledged as asymmetrical, is theorised as one of exchange in all directions. We are reminded that all those involved in the colonial encounter were both actors and acted upon.

However, for the Western imperialists it has always been about circulation, not primarily of ideas but circulation as trade, and very much on their

---

[13] www.lemonde.fr/idees/article/2018/11/25/restitution-du-patrimomine-africain-le-signe-d-un-pillage-present_5388326_3232.html.

terms. The 1897 sacking of the Oba's palace in Benin was itself largely caused because of the frustration of the British who felt their access to new West African markets was were being blocked (Coombes, 1997, 8–28). Fixity only happened after conquest, once relationships were fixed in favour of the colonial powers.

Consequently, it is the very fixity of current ownership arrangements that are at the heart of repatriation debates. If circulation were truly a goal for Western museums, they would long ago have been actively participating in lending collections to museums in the Global South. For example, at the time of the 1977 FESTAC Second World Black and African Festival of Arts and Culture festival in Lagos, Nigeria, the British Museum refused the loan of an ivory mask, a portrait of Queen Idia of Benin. The mask had been chosen as the official emblem of the festival.

A *Washington Post* article written at the time explained that of the four known copies of the mask (all dated to the first half of the sixteenth century) the one held by British Museum is the finest example. Due to the lack of loan, a copy of the mask was commissioned by the Nigerian Ministry of Information from the artist Felix Idubor who had to work within difficult constraints:

> Although he has been to London, Idubor said he never has seen the original mask, which caused him some problems in reproducing it. "You don't see the back or the hair, only the front view on the postcard," he said. "You have to put in a lot of imaginations."[14]

The constraints faced by Idubor are the same as those faced by many artists working in West Africa today, namely a lack of direct access to their cultural heritage. As Derrida (1995) states, the violence of the archive is often what it excludes. Another form of violence is disenfranchising those who have the most to gain from access. Yet the retrieval dimension of the archive is usually under-theorised, archives sometimes existing seemingly only to amass. This is not true of the colonial archive, which was a political project of domination and justification, an archive 'performed' at European Colonial Exhibitions, then recycled to form the founding collections of many of the museums of Europe (De L'Estoile, 2010).

By reflecting on the 1977 rejected loan request, it seems clear that the British Museum has long known of the importance of Benin royal objects for the ongoing cultural, spiritual, economic and creative health of Benin City yet has chosen not to take steps to rectify the situation. The harm of retention has been

---

[14] www.washingtonpost.com/archive/lifestyle/1977/02/11/the-controversial-mask-of-benin /f6845f66-ffbd-40e5-8bc4-b7a551bdb8d0/?utm_term=.e7235060bdda (accessed 17/06/19).

set out by representatives of the Benin royal family, academics, historians and artists for generations.

In her paper *Making Meaning from a Fragmented Past: 1897 and the creative process*, Peju Layiwola (2014), a Nigerian artist related to the Benin Royal Family explores the importance of the events of the 1897 plundering of the Oba's Palace and its constant echoes through Nigerian art ever since:

> Like a cancerous sore, the 1897 historical episode keeps recurring and continually elicits responses from advocates of repatriation of cultural arte-facts in Nigeria and across the globe. It has therefore not only become a reference point in the discourse of imperialism in Africa with several incidences of pillaging in other parts of the continent, but also forms a specifically disturbing legacy of British Benin imperial encounter which the West can no longer negate, but has to come to terms with. (88)

Layiwola documents many African artists reactions to 1897 including installations, novels, cartoons, plays and films. While 1897 may not mean much to a British public, the date has huge significance for a Nigerian one, for example:

> *Benin1897.com: Art and the Restitution Question*, a travelling exhibition, was shown in Lagos ... and later in Ibadan. In its four months of showing time in Nigeria, it generated a lot of discussions and provided insights into how a historical work can open up various streams of thoughts ... The title's pun from cyber language on the '.com', the commercial domain name, became a metaphor for the overwhelming economic interest of the British in the sacking of Benin. Rather than follow the official history, which plays up the ambush of a British party on an alleged mission to appeal to the king of Benin to keep with the terms of an agreement over trade, the exhibition fully expresses the often suppressed intent of the British to plunder Benin a year before the Massacre. (90)

Layiwola then describes the work of Osaigbovo Agbonzee, who goes by the stage name Monday Midnite and creates films bringing together images of the Oba in exile after the Massacre with the current British Royal family including contemporary events such as the 2012 wedding between Prince William and Catherine Middleton or the terrorist attacks in London in July 2005. Monday Midnite is asking questions about temporality and proximity: about the way in which the lives of the descendants of the royal family who benefited from the 1897 looting are inextricably linked to the lives of the descendants of the Oba who are living without. He is asking questions about the nature of violence – of blood spilt – and the way in which some violence is validated and other forms repudiated. Similarly, the cartoonist and academic Ganiyu Jimoh references iconic civil rights moments to contextualise repatriation debates in his work (see figure 2).

Figure 2 Cartoon by Ganiyu A. Jimoh (Jimga) entitled 'Riot' (2011)

So whereas the return of the Benin Bronzes, seen from a UK perspective, is about legal convention (it would take an act of parliament to allow the British Museum to de-accession its collection), about future trade relationship between the UK and Nigeria and about the potential loss to a cosmopolitan, universal art history canon, in Nigeria it is about social justice and a continuation of the global civil rights movement. The return of the Benin Bronzes would allow future generations to have meaningful access to their artistic and cultural archive of which they feel dispossessed.

These same arguments, about the importance of culture for wellbeing can be found in the 2017 UK Department for Digital, Culture, Media and Sports (DCMS) commissioned the Mendoza Review of UK Museums:

> There is increasing evidence to show that cultural institutions contribute a great deal to the local economy, to the wellbeing and education of its residents, and to attracting tourists and businesses to the area. Museums are especially able to do this because of their position as a civic space and their collections, *which connect people to place.* (2017: 10, my emphasis)

The connection of people to place, of people to their past through material forms that endure beyond the life span of individuals is a founding principle of museums. It seems a strange anomaly therefore that arguments that are used by Western museums to justify their ongoing relevance and government funding are not being accepted as valid when coming from other parts of the world.

Entanglement As Moral Abdication

Another dimension to the evocation of 'entanglement' in relation to repatriation claims is one that could be described as a moral ambiguity, as a bracketing off of judgement about what happened to whom and under what conditions of consent or coercion. For example, the term 'entanglement' is not deployed in relation to Nazi looted art, this is because few would be willing to attempt a moral case for retention. The story of the Holocaust is 'known' by all, and as such routes to justice are clear.

Claims for restitution of African material culture on the other hand can be described as unravelling claims, unravelling towards narratives that are not yet fixed. The European coloniser is still for many heritage professionals an ambiguous figure, at some points one that should be judged by 'the intellectual landscape at the time' and at others disavowed as a brutal male oppressor. Ambiguity around this persona causes ambiguity about the museum's current relationship with its collections.

In a different way, the demand of the return of the Parthenon Friezes does not lead scholars to invoke entanglement but instead claims of proximity, part of a familiar narrative about a common European identity. The debate is contested but operates within reassuring identity claims of the roots of European identity, even if in 2019 the symbolism of these common roots is being severely strained by the UK's attempts to leave the European Union. The UK's desire to leave the EU has been pointed out by Greek officials who would like to borrow the Parthenon Friezes held in the British Museum in time for their display in Athens in 2021 to commemorate the 200th anniversary of the start of the war of independence against the Ottoman Empire.[15] Once again, the condition of a loan from the British Museum rests upon a demand for the Greek Government to accept UK ownership first.

The British Museum's stance of retention of the Parthenon Friezes is out of step with public opinion in the UK, where polls consistently show a majority of UK citizens think they should be returned to Greece (cf. Robertson, 2019). Emmanuel Macron, perhaps a more astute judge of cultural politics, has agreed to lend Athens the fragments of Parthenon Frieze that have been in the Louvre Museum for the past 200 years.[16] Both the British Museum and the Louvre have been offered loans of other Greek objects, previously unseen outside Greece, in return for the loan of the Parthenon Friezes in what was a very carefully worded diplomatic request from Athens.[17]

The playing out of repatriation claims is therefore both constitutive of and dependent upon the wider political reckoning with colonial pasts. The generational shift that can be discerned in relation to return of objects is part of a broader societal shift towards the recognition (by younger generations) of the brutality of colonialism. The nostalgia for an airbrushed version of colonial European identity is slipping away, to be replaced with a sobering reckoning with the catastrophic nature of colonial legacies. The fact that objects taken during colonial conflict were exempt from international conventions is increasingly being seen as an error of judgement at the time, not a legal loophole:

> It is generally accepted by legal scholars that a custom that protected cultural objects during war began to develop around 1815. This development continued until it was finally codified at the end of the nineteenth century in an international convention on the rules of warfare, agreed to by 51 countries at the Hague, Netherlands in 1899 . . . It is a cruel twist of fate that the pillage of Benin City, resulting in what was probably the greatest haul of African artwork in history, took place two years before the Hague Convention was signed. And it seems patently unfair that a principle which had been applied between European states more or less since 1815 was dead in the water when it came to Africa – or any other colonised territory for that matter. . . . while the looting of African stores was not legally forbidden at the time, the actions were nonetheless of questionable morality, even back then. To use the language of the 1880 Oxford Manual, it still violated the 'principles of justice which guide the public conscience'.[18]

---

[15] www.telegraph.co.uk/news/2019/09/03/greece-has-acknowledge-british-museum-ownership-wants-loan-elgin/.

[16] www.theartnewspaper.com/news/louvre-in-talks-to-loan-parthenon-frieze-to-greece.

[17] www.theguardian.com/culture/2019/aug/31/greece-sculpture-swap-athens-partheon-elgin-marbles-boris-johnson.

[18] https://ial.uk.com/law-restitution-and-the-benin-bronzes/.

Principles of justice have therefore always existed in parallel to the laws at any given time. Repatriation claims do not, as some people claim, rely on applying today's moral norms to a very different past as moral norms have always been heterogenous and contested and laws have not always reflected popular opinion.

Attribution and 'Truth'

One of the most difficult decisions facing museum curators confronted with repatriation claims is how to frame the concept of 'scientific knowledge' in a way that does not further alienate communities who have been dispossessed of their heritage. The case of the 'Gweagal Shield', a shield displayed in the British Museum and thought until recently to have been acquired by Captain Cook during his first encounter with Australian Aboriginal people in Botany Bay in April 1770, is one such example.

In two papers published in 2018 (Thomas; Nugent & Sculthorpe) the 'case of identity' of the shield is explored in relation to historical, archival and scientific research. Until 2016, the somewhat shaky identity of the shield held in the British Museum (label faded and uncertain attribution) was put aside in favour of a clear narrative: the shield closely enough resembled the shield thought to have been collected by Captain Cook. The evidence used was an illustration by John Frederick Miller in 1771 and its proximity to other objects collected during the Botany Bay expedition. The Shield was labelled and displayed as such in the British Museum and spoken about by the then Director of the museum, Neil McGregor, as part of his *A History of the World in One Hundred Objects'* BBC Radio 4 series in 2010. In a confident tone, he narrates:

> We know the precise date that it (the shield) came in to Cooks' hands, the 29 April 1770, we have written accounts of the day from Cook himself. But the indigenous Australian who owned the shield did not write, and this is why a history told from objects can be so important. For the unnamed man confronting his first European on the shore of Botany Bay nearly 250 years ago, this shield is his lasting statement. (McGregor, 2010: 490)

Given this framing, it is unsurprising that on the occasion of the shield's display in Australia in 2016 as part of the *Encounter* exhibition at the National Museum in Canberra, a repatriation claim was made by Rodney Kelly, a Dharawal and Yuin man from New South Wales who claimed that the shield belonged to his great-great-great-great-great-great grandfather,

Cooman.[19] His claim gained political support from the New South Wales Green Senator and Kelly has since made visits to the British Museum to visit the shield and press his case.

Since 2016, further archival and scientific research has brought the shield's identity in to question. Thomas (2018) notes the discrepancy between the shield and the illustration, and scientific analysis has found that the hole in the shield could not have been made by a musket bullet as had been previously thought, but most likely from a spear (potentially during ceremonial use). The shield was also found to be made out of wood that came from a region 500 kilometres from Botany Bay. Thomas suggests a number of ways in which the shield could have entered the British Museum collection and a number of fates that could have befallen the shield collected by Cook. This recent research was met with scepticism by Kelly who notes the fact that the research was only undertaken after the repatriation claim was made. In their paper, Nugent and Sculthorpe comment:

> Basic object and collection research like this remains a crucial aspect of museum work, even though it tends to be criticized by those who argue that empiricism and connoisseurship are a continuation of the museum's 'enlightenment' origins and out of keeping with contemporary efforts to decolonise imperial and colonial institutions (2018: 42)

In defence of Kelly's position, he became aware of the shield as presented in 2016 and as narrated by Neil McGregor. Given this, and the fact that the shield was collected during colonial contact, it is not surprising that a change of story would not change his claim. The status of the 'scientific' knowledge that presented the shield as that collected by Cook is the same as the science that says it is not – namely open to future revision. In the recent writings about the shield, none of the authors make assertions as to what these new findings mean in relation to the repatriation claim, instead they suggest that things are inevitably more complicated than they first appear. However, it is this very turn to complexity which paralyses many claims and makes claimants feel disempowered in a system that they feel is stacked against them.

Kelly's moral claim to the shield can be theorised as an 'interruption' in the story the British Museum has been telling about the object. This moral dimension can be broken down in to three constitutive parts:

1. The shield was taken during a time of conflict (*coercion*)
2. The British Museum retains control of the display and interpretation (*alienation*)

---

[19] www.smh.com.au/world/europe/the-gripping-story-of-the-gweagal-shield-20190511-p51mbe.html.

3. Past atrocities are being felt in the present through local and global structural inequalities and discrimination set in motion at the time the shield was taken (*ongoing despair*).

While ostensibly made on behalf of Gweagal communities, Kelly's claim is not officially supported by everyone who could bring claims such as the 'Gweagal families group' or the La Perouse Local Area Land Council.[20] The definition of 'descendent community' and evaluation of who has the right to make cultural claims on behalf of different past peoples is very often contested. This is due to the complexities of history, national boundaries (drawn and redrawn), definitions of descent (biological, cultural, social, political, economic, religious, artistic, gendered, existential and so on) and abilities for individuals or communities to be 'heard' within a recognised heritage discourse (cf. Smith, 2006 on a Foucauldian notion of power that leads to an authorised heritage discourse within which certain voices are drowned out). This complexity alone is enough to lead some heritage professionals to consider any form of repatriation/restitution an impossibility, a constructed political fantasy in the present that more often than not enters the realm of 'invented traditions' (Hobsbawn & Ranger, 1983) or 'imagined communities' (Anderson, 1983) as projects of contemporary nationalism.

On the other hand, the fact that the shield indexes the triad of coercion, alienation and ongoing despair can be seen to give Kelly's claim a moral authority beyond that of the curator/scientist. It seems that only in conditions where the museum could robustly help to address these grievances could a scenario be envisaged where the museum becomes part of the solution, restoring a voice to those who feel disenfranchised. A turn to archival and scientific research is not an adequate answer to a question about dignity unless it includes the concerns of those who have brought the claim as a key catalyst to the research.

Many museums would argue that they are already a part of a solution to ongoing marginalisation and point to a broad range of positive engagements between museums and indigenous Australian communities that have taken place over the last few decades. It is true that museums in Australia and Europe have been both advocates and supporters of indigenous representation and claims and, through showcasing Maori and indigenous Australian heritage and contemporary art internationally have leveraged campaigns within the countries concerned and materially helped to support the careers of a number of indigenous practitioners.

---

[20] Personal Communication, Professor Nicholas Thomas, August 2019.

Scientific and Aesthetic Collecting

While the return of objects taken during violent conflict has entered a new ethical realm, the Macron report also indicated that restitution claims should be considered in the case of ethnographic missions, such as the Dakar-Djibouti expedition undertaken between 1931 and 1933. However, the harm done by these missions was considered by Macron of second order:

> While praising the work of the two scholars, the French President clearly also distanced himself from their most controversial points. In the first round of restitutions, scheduled for 2019, Macron did not include items obtained by ethnographic missions, as had been requested by Savoy and Sarr.[21]

As described earlier, the relationships of power under colonial conditions meant that although violence was not always directly involved on ethnographic missions, bribery, coercion and threatened violence were certainly present. Additionally, the collecting missions themselves were informed by a deeply problematic way of 'knowing' others through their material life. De L'Estoile explains:

> The Dakar-Djibouti expedition therefore appears to be the equivalent for French ethnography of the voyages of discovery by scientists in previous centuries, the best known of whom is (Charles) Darwin. (2010: 189, my translation)

De L'Estoile goes on to explore how the 'scientific' ethnographic collectors of the colonial expeditions set themselves apart from 'aesthetic' collectors of foreign objects. They saw their mission as akin to that of 'scientific archaeologists', piecing together knowledge about societies through painstaking and systematic collecting. The anthropological canon at the time was still largely influenced by ideas of cultural evolutionism (inspired by Darwin's theory of natural selection) so the objects collected were used to tell a story of progress, from African primitivism to European modernity.

While this story of the European 'civilising' mission has largely collapsed under scrutiny of the violent de-humanisation of the colonial encounter and a reckoning with two World Wars, the logic of the 'progress story' remains the organising principle of many ethnographic museum collections in the West. It can be seen in the categories used to describe and label objects, for example, the Pitt-Rivers Museum, adopted by museums across the UK (see figure 3).

---

[21] www.theartnewspaper.com/news/french-president-emmanuel-macron-calls-for-international-conference-on-the-return-of-african-artefacts.

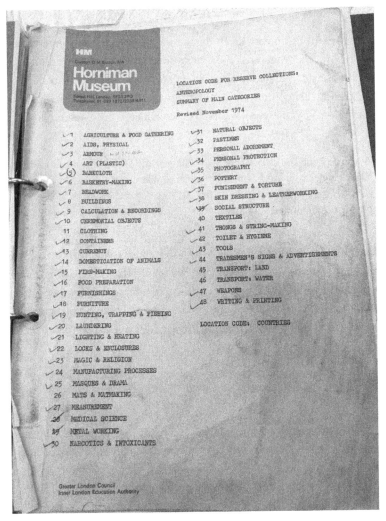

Figure 3 'Summary of Main Categories' used for storage and archive purposes at the Horniman Museum in 2019. The document was last updated in 1974.

The logic of a story of cultural progress has therefore created a form of sedimentary racism that museum professionals now spend their time trying to excavate. As the layers are uncovered and new exhibitions and new curators provide different interpretations, it is hoped that the ordering logic that brought ethnographic collections together can be undone. However, these new configurations take place within the restraints of the museum's overarching ordering power. Unlike art residencies and outreach programmes that seem doomed to continually reinscribe the same power relations within slight variations, the repatriation of objects is one of the few acts that could meaningfully reconfigure power relations and lead to new ethical relationships.

Instead of embracing these possibilities, it seems that there is a fear that the repatriation of certain objects will 'open the floodgates' and see museums emptied of their collections, a scenario in which a reverse engineering of the colonial encounter leads the West back to itself and the curators end up alone, in empty museums, no longer able to say anything about 'the other' and perhaps barely able to say much about themselves.

Given the tens of thousands of potentially contested objects held by museums worldwide, repatriation negotiations have become a permanent reality for Western curators. The traditional skill set of curators is shifting towards outward facing diplomatic abilities in order to deal with highly emotionally charged challenges to the museum's authority. As the museum workforce diversifies and a generational shift orientates new curators towards notions of justice as much as custodianship, it can be hoped that repatriation cases are dealt with in new and open ways and seen as positive opportunities not moments of loss. In July 2019, after the latest meeting of the Benin Dialogue Group, this time held in Benin City, a press release announced:

> The Benin Dialogue Group acknowledges the looting of Benin in 1897 and understands that many of the museum collections were assembled as a result of this event. Acknowledging the deep loss that this event caused, the members of the Benin Dialogue Group shared knowledge regarding various initiatives across Europe that are currently seeking to address the questions of return and restitution. There are national, international and institutional legal complexities that govern issues of return and restitution particularly as member museums are from different countries and jurisdictions with different laws and regulations. The Benin Dialogue Group will continue to share information and keep partners updated on changes and provide support in this continuing conversation.[22]

By embracing a language that includes the concept of loss and considers ideas of restitution and return, the first step towards what can be hoped will be full return has been taken. The western participants have not yet fully removed their safety harnesses of 'legal complexities' or security blankets of 'laws and regulations' yet seem willing to start to reframe heritage as justice.

---

[22] www.tropenmuseum.nl/nl/press-statement-meeting-benin-dialogue-group-1 (accessed 12/01/2020).

Case by Case?

Are repatriation claims, such as the case of Benin Bronzes, truly about individual cases or a much bigger political truth? How many of the museum professionals participating in the Benin Dialogue Group are also thinking about the Parthenon Friezes held in the British Museum or their Egyptian collections or collections still hidden from public scrutiny? Are some cases given the time and attention they deserve because of the political zeitgeist and others overlooked? How can a museum or nation develop an ethical framework within which to think through repatriation cases in relation to heritage justice and future generations? Most importantly, how can the ethical framework avoid being about Western museums and their need to address their postcolonial identity and instead be meaningfully focussed on those people making the claims?

It is true that the very legitimacy of the museum as an institution is being questioned by these dialogues. And yet, it seems both empowering and hopeful that museums should and can question their past and their collections. Individual museums can probably navigate their own ethical journeys more easily than state led initiative, yet to date have operated in the shadow of state level legislation. The Museum Association's code of ethics includes the commitment to:

> 2.5. Reject any item for purchase, loan or donation if there is any suspicion that it was wrongfully taken during a time of conflict, stolen, illicitly exported or illicitly traded, unless explicitly allowed by treaties or other agreements, or where the museum is co-operating with attempts to establish the identity of the rightful owner(s) of an item.[23]

Beyond this commitment to future collecting, most museums are actively undertaking a review of their collections that were 'wrongfully taken' within a political climate that is continuously expanding the category of what is considered 'wrongful'. As will be discussed in 'Justice As International Law', the efforts of the International Criminal Court to end impunity in the face of crimes against cultural heritage necessitates State Parties to sign up to a 'Guarantee of Non-Recurrence'. This guarantee is a commitment to tackle the structural and political conditions that led to the violence in the first place. As will be explored, if adapted to museums, the principle could provide a route-map for ethical collecting practice and dealing with contested collections with a focus on creating new structural relationships and political conditions that prevent future cultural crimes.

---

[23] www.museumsassociation.org/home.

Justice As International Law

When designing the permanent premises of the International Criminal Court, the aim was to communicate trust, hope and – most importantly – faith in justice and fairness. The building requires the courage to be an ambassador for the credibility and values of the ICC. The project and its architecture are impressive and grand in scale but always relate to humans and the human scale. It is important that a formal institution like the ICC does not constitute barriers for people. On the contrary, it expresses the very essence of democratic architecture
(description of the ICC project by Danish architects Schmidt, Hammer & Lessen)

The Staging of Justice

The International Criminal Court was established in July 2002 by international treaty, with the participation of 122 State Parties.[24] The crimes the ICC has been set up to try are the crimes that have impact on a global scale: war crimes, crimes against humanity, genocide and crimes of aggression (the use of state military force in contravention with the UN Charter of 1945). The ICC building is located in The Hague, Netherlands and has field offices around the world, mostly in Africa. Its budget for 2019 was €148,135,100 which pays for 800 staff and the running of the court. Since its inception in 2002, the court has dealt with twenty-seven cases, predominantly in Africa.

The court is made up of The Presidency (an elected president and two Vice-presidents), The Office of the Prosecutor (OTP) whose mandate it is to decide whether to investigate referred cases, The Divisions (eighteen judges who work in one of three sections – Pre-Trial, Trial and Appeals) and the Registry, responsible for much of the day to day running of the court. The court as a whole is overseen by the Assembly of States Parties (ASP) made up of signatories to the Rome Statute that established the court in 2002 (first drafted in 1998).[25]

The architecture of the ICC embodies the principle of visibility through its use of glass and water. It also feels like it is arranged as a process, from outside chaos to internal calm. Having entered the building through formal security airport-like procedures, you step on to a bridge over a canal of still water and into the main building. There are the usual high ceilings, flags of the State Parties and to the left, behind the main reception desk, a garden (one of four in the building, this one the Africa Garden) which is not accessible to the public. A museum-like installation in the foyer explains the work of the court through a series of installations.

---

[24] In 2019 the state parties were made up of thirty-three from Africa, eighteen from Asia Pacific, eighteen from Eastern Europe, twenty-eight from Latin America and the Caribbean and twenty-five from Western Europe and North America.

[25] www.icc-cpi.int/resource-library/documents/rs-eng.pdf (accessed 10 September 2019).

In fact, the whole court is set up as a public space, to be visited by the citizens of the world that the court is trying to bring into being. These include school parties, public interest groups, NGOs, journalists and politicians. It is a solemn space, punctuated by the muted tones of visitors or the lively confident conversation of the many interns (identifiable through their wearing of lanyards). The café space is open to the public and serves drinks and cold food. While the staff canteen is off-bounds and housed in the private part of the court, hot food can be ordered from it and brought down to be public café. This overlapping of private and public spaces makes the court feel hospitable and serves to reduce the feeling of hierarchy between the court employees and the ordinary citizen.

Journalists are crucial to the success of the ICC as the court relies on public dissemination of its work for its ongoing legitimacy and funding. They are therefore carefully catered for through a designated press room and given access to frequently updated press releases, databanks of images and interviews with key ICC personnel. For example, during the Al Mahdi trial in 2016 concerning the destruction of protected religious sites in Timbuktu (discussed below), journalists from Mali were looked after by an ICC employee who greeted them in French, kept them up to date with the court's timetabling and ensured they had everything they needed to file their stories.

The court viewing area, accessed after another round of security checks, consist of rows of seats designed to separate different publics: those there on behalf of the prosecution, defence, NGOs, journalists and politicians. The seats at the back are available to the general public. Headphones with simultaneous translation into the court's working languages (French, English and in the case of the Al Mahdi trial, Arabic) are provided and court officials walk up and down the room ensuring that court protocol is followed (rising for the judges and so on). The viewing area is separated by a vast glass screen from the court itself and a curtain is lowered when the case is adjourned or has to go in to closed session. The whole proceedings are broadcast on webcams and can therefore be watched in real time from anywhere in the world (with a thirty-minute delay).

The staging of justice at the ICC feels controlled, forensic and theatrical. The judges and court clerks wear the uniform of Western legal courts, whereas the defendants may not. For example, at the confirmation of charges hearing of Al-Hassan in May 2019, he chose to wear traditional Tuareg clothing in contrast to the sombre suits of the court.

This sartorial choice is a small glimpse of a wider conflict going on between the court and its critics. As will be explored, the legitimacy of the court is not universally recognised and like many Western institutions, it has been accused of being asymmetrical in its dealings with war crimes and crimes against humanity (Ogunfolu & Assim, 2012). For critics, the fact that the vast majority of cases currently under investigation concern Africa is testimony to the court's inability to hold more powerful states to account (see figure 4).

Figure 4 Exhibition in the foyer of the International Criminal Court in the Hague, 2019. The exhibition takes the visitor on an idealised journey through the work of the ICC.

Justice As a Process

The installation/museum housed in the entrance lobby of the court is designed as a process of hope, a process which is able to contain even the most violently dehumanising acts and translate them in to justice and dignity for the victim.

The first space, entitled 'Towards a More Just World' shows four large screens of people talking about harrowing events (subtitled but without sound, some not even subtitled).

Three of the four films are shot in Africa. The common theme is arbitrary violence, rape and destruction muted out against defenceless, unsuspecting people. They recall the attacks in bewildered, broken or angry speech, seemingly addressing themselves to the world (to us, the viewers) – how could this have happened to us? To our children?

In the middle of the installation is a suspended sepia cube showing an artist's outline of a woman's head – the same woman that can be seen in every subsequent installation, presumably an outline of the 'universal human subject' going through the process of finding justice via the ICC.

The second installation is entitled 'Rome Statute 1998' and has a panel with a film about the ICC in statistical graphs. Under the screen are four drawers that can be pulled out to reveal printed text on board – the drawers are each labelled with a different crime: Genocide, Crimes against Humanity, War Crime and Crimes of Aggression – and the text printed on board is the formal description of the crime. Underneath the four drawers is a large single drawer labelled 'Rome Statute' and pulling it out reveals the text of the treaty.

The next installation sets out the ICC process and a map of where it operates. A desk with a computer and blank files is set up for you to be able to sit down and imagine yourself carrying out the preliminary research or investigations. Behind is a wall featuring outreach and sensitisation initiatives, illustrated by photographs of assembled people and some objects: a drum, a radio and a loudspeaker. Then, you walk through a tent like structure of suspended white sheets on to which some testimonies of victims have been written – most of the sheets are blank however, presumably for testimonies still to come, an unsettling insight in to the fact that the world still contains countless potential acts of violent dehumanisation.

The next room has an 'evidence wall' made up of empty crime scene bags, a very large metal case used in the field to contain bagged evidence, a stack of A4 box files with colour coded labels and examples of sorts of evidence found – including a blood-stained knife. A large label declares that evidence is stored in 'the vault' (presumably somewhere in close proximity to the ICC). Beyond this you can sit at a desk and imagine yourself giving evidence into a microphone – your pixelated face visible on a screen beneath you. To your left is a large glass case containing the ICC judge robes and in front of you are five screens set out as they would be in court on which you can see the representatives of the victims, the prosecution team, the judges, the defence team and the registry.

The final room is the court in action, including the film of a young African woman giving her evidence. She is visibly distressed as she is asked 'after all that has happened to you, how do you feel?' and she answers: 'In my community I am no longer considered a human being'. She is defiant yet distressed, broken by gender-based violence in body and spirit.

As you leave, you are urged to participate in the awareness-building mission of the ICC by taking a photograph of yourself with the criminal court logo behind you – these photos are then posted on social media and include many visitors smiling in an incongruous manner. You can also record and upload a short oral testimony. Some screens of photos and films are hung alongside these interactive booths including one of young people wearing 'restoring hope to victims' t-shirts and a short film with people being fitted with artificial limbs.

What Did Al-Mahdi Destroy?

In the same way that museum repatriation cases are linked morally and conceptually to one another within a common logic of materiality and dignity, the successful trial of Al-Mahdi by the ICC is linked to the ongoing performative destruction of cultural heritage by radical Islamic groups:

> During the trial, Fatou Bensouda, the ICC's chief prosecutor, compared the attacks in Timbuktu to Islamic State's recent destruction of monuments in the Syrian city of Palmyra and the Taliban's wrecking of the Bamiyan Buddha statues in Afghanistan in 2001. It is unlikely that anyone from Iraq and Syria, where archaeological sites have been systematically damaged and ransacked for artifacts over recent years, will find themselves in the dock in The Hague any time soon. Neither country is a signatory to the ICC's founding Rome statute, meaning that without a mandate from the UN security council an ICC investigation into such crimes is not yet possible.[26]

The Ahmad Al Faqi Al Mahdi (Al Mahdi) case concerned the ordered destruction of nine mausoleums and the door of the Sidi Yahia mosque in Timbuktu in 2012. At the time of the destruction, Al-Mahdi was allegedly head of the 'Hesba' (morality police) in the town and a key agent in the imposition of a strict form of Shari'a law (including ordering stonings, amputations, forced marriages, imposing strict dress and behaviour codes and the banning of music, smoking, alcohol and sport). The ICC chose to limit its prosecution against Al Mahdi to the destruction of protected sites because it felt it needed to act against the global rise in performative destruction by radical Islamists (in Afghanistan, Iraq, Syria and so on). To many victims of the occupation of Timbuktu, this was disappointing as they would have liked Al-Mahdi to have been put on trial for all of his alleged crimes, however the ICC judged this to be potentially too risky. The Al-Mahdi trial was therefore an essential act of assertion on behalf of the ICC against impunity in the face of destruction of global heritage.

The choice of buildings to destroy in Timbuktu was calculated to cause maximum harm and humiliation. The door of the Sidi Yahia Mosque has particular symbolic importance because it was believed that the destruction of the door would mark the end of the world. Importantly for the ICC and

---

[26] www.theguardian.com/world/2016/sep/27/timbuktu-shrines-icc-sentences-islamic-militant-nine-years-destruction-ahmad-al-faqi-al-mahdi.

UNESCO (and by logical consequence the international community) eight of these Protected Buildings had been declared World Heritage sites by UNESCO in 1988 due their unique architectural merit and the role of Timbuktu as a centre of learning, essential for the spread of Islam across West Africa during the town's Golden Age in the sixteenth Century. Timbuktu, informally known as the 'town of 333 Saints' was a logical focus for the attack by radical Islamists in 2012 as they believe that the worshiping of Saints is an idolatrous act. The synchretic Islam found in much of Mali (involving petitionary prayer, sacrifices, the wearing of amulets and so on) is regarded by Salafi Muslims as 'haram' (forbidden) and a sign of superstition. The destruction of the tombs and in particular the door of the Sidi Yahia mosque was therefore an act of purification, a way to show the population of Timbuktu that their devotionary practices were superstitious and wrong.

The Universality of the ICC?

In *Fictions of Justice: The International Criminal Court and the Challenge of Legal Pluralism in Sub-Saharan Africa*, Clarke (2009) takes exception with the ICC's framing of victimhood and what she terms 'the international NGOs donor capitalists' intervention in traditional legal systems in sub-Saharan Africa. The heart of her argument is that fundamentally different (incommensurable) world views, such as a world governed by Shari'a law, should be accommodated within a 'universalistic' vision of human rights, such as that embodied by the ICC. Unfortunately, her call for true 'legal plurality' is as difficult in one direction as a pure 'scientific rational' view is in the other. The international understanding of human rights, victimhood, adulthood and redemption found at the ICC is focussed on the body and suffering.

The example given by Clarke, one of a Nigerian woman sentenced to death by stoning by a Shari'a court for having a child out of wedlock, is not for the ICC worthy of nuancing or framing within a different world view. Clarke suggests that this could be judged as a failure of humanist imagination, a misguided emphasis on lived human suffering against the bigger picture of spiritual redemption. Another example given by Clarke is that of the amputated hand of someone found guilty of theft under Shari'a law, the hand goes to hell while the rest of the person's body is purified. However, it is hard to see how such a perspective could be incorporated into the vision of the ICC as the court takes as its founding principle the upholding of the dignity of the individual human subject. In fact, at the trial of Al Mahdi in 2015, no defence of 'different world view' was put forward in order to explain his acts. Instead, he pleaded guilty and apologised in a carefully scripted speech that meant that his sentence was reduced to nine years in prison (against a potential thirty-year sentence):

> I am really sorry. I am really remorseful, and I regret all the damage that my actions have caused. I regret what I have caused to my family, my community in Timbuktu, what I have caused my home nation, Mali, and I'm really remorseful about what I had caused the international community as a whole. My regret is directly – or, is directed particularly to the generations, the ancestors of the holders of the mausoleums that I have destroyed. I would like to seek their pardon, I would like to seek the pardon of the whole people of Timbuktu, I would like to make them a solemn promise that this was the first and the last wrongful act I will ever commit. I seek their forgiveness and I would like them to look at me as a son that has lost his way and consider me part of the social fabric of Timbuktu and must not forget what I have contributed in the past to Timbuktu. It is my hope that in accordance with the noble Islamic principles to be able to forgive me and to accept my regret ... If I was influenced by a group of deviant people from Al-Qaeda and Ansar Dine, and if they were able to influence me, to carry me in their evil wave through actions that affected the whole population, but even with these temporary actions I do not think that we will be able to change the heritage of the city of Timbuktu.[27]

In 2018, Al Mahdi was moved to a prison in Scotland to complete his sentence. In a press release about the transfer the ICC stated: 'The ICC relies on state support at the enforcement of sentence stage and is highly appreciative of the voluntary cooperation of the Scottish and United Kingdom Governments in respect of Mr Al Mahdi'.[28] International law facilitated the arrest of Al-Mahdi in Niger after fleeing Mali, his transfer to the Hague for trial and now his imprisonment in Scotland, a global response to a localised act of cultural destruction.

Crimes against People and Crimes against Buildings

The context of the 2015 trial against Al-Mahdi was the destabilisation of Mali in 2012 by a Tuareg-led uprising in the North and a military coup against the government in the capital, Bamako. Violence against people and protected sites quickly followed. In July 2012, the Malian government referred the case to the ICC, covering events from January 2012 with no end date. Mali had ratified the Rome Statute in 2000. The ICC went on to define what it considered was its responsibility after an initial assessment of the situation:

---

[27] www.icc-cpi.int/mali/al-mahdi/Documents/Al-Mahdi-Admission-of-guilt-transcript-ENG.pdf.
[28] www.icc-cpi.int/Pages/item.aspx?name=pr1451.

The information available indicates that there is a reasonable basis to believe that war crimes have been committed in Mali since January 2012, namely: (1) murder constituting war crime under Article 8(2)(c)(i); (2) the passing of sentences and the carrying out of executions without due process constituting war crime under Article 8(2)(c)(iv); (3) mutilation, cruel treatment and torture constituting war crimes under Article 8(2)(c)(i); (4) intentionally directing attacks against protected objects constituting war crimes under Article 8(2)(e)(iv); (5) pillaging constituting war crime under Article 8(2) (e)(v); and (6) rape constituting war crimes under Article 8(2)(e)(vi).[29]

The ICC's containment of horror happens immediately by dividing crimes into categories and tagging them to particular detailed descriptions described in the different articles of the Rome Statute. For example, the detail of intentionally directing attacks against protected objects is broken down further in a document entitled 'elements of crimes':

Article 8 (2) (b) (ix)War crime of attacking protected objects
Elements:

1. The perpetrator directed an attack.
2. The object of the attack was one or more buildings dedicated to religion, education, art, science or charitable purposes, historic monuments, hospitals or places where the sick and wounded are collected, which were not military objectives.
3. The perpetrator intended such building or buildings dedicated to religion, education, art, science or charitable purposes, historic monuments, hospitals or places where the sick and wounded are collected, which were not military objectives, to be the object of the attack.
4. The conduct took place in the context of and was associated with an international armed conflict.
5. The perpetrator was aware of factual circumstances that established the existence of an armed conflict.[30]

The ICC's logic in evaluating what is and is not a crime is therefore set out for all to see, cut down into detail and further detail. In the courtroom, these definitions are debated in relation to particular cases, for example, the length of a conflict for it to be regarded as deliberate rather than sporadic. Through the Rome Statute, the ICC has the right to bracket off events and scrutinise them through a lens of dignity and violence perpetrated against individual bodies and individual sites. The nature of the damage to the individual bodies and sites, the

---

[29] www.icc-cpi.int/itemsDocuments/SASMaliArticle53_1PublicReportENG16Jan2013.pdf.

[30] www.icc-cpi.int/resource-library/Documents/ElementsOfCrimesEng.pdf. Elements of Crime Published by the International Criminal Court ISBN No. 92-9227-232-2 ICC-PIOS-LT-03-002/15_Eng Copyright © International Criminal Court 2013 All rights reserved International Criminal Court | Po Box 19519 | 2500 CM | The Hague | The Netherlands | www.icc-cpi.int.

material harm, is exposed, defined and refined to allow for a full account of harm suffered and ongoing trauma. Once the extent of the trauma is established, the reparation phase of the trial is set in motion, through the work of the Trust Fund for Victims.

Reparations

The work of the Trust Fund for Victims (TFV) consists of establishing the extent of the impact of crimes on victims in order to set fair reparations. The logic of the reparations is one of both symbolism and proportionality. For example, after pleading guilty, Al Mahdi was ordered to pay one symbolic euro to the Government of Mali through UNESCO. This symbolic act was made possible by Al Mahdi's apology which was felt by the ICC to be sincere and hoped to have a positive effect on discouraging future acts of violent destruction. Other factors taken in to account by the TFV were the collapse of tourism in the region, the loss of revenue to the families who derived an income from controlling access to the destroyed Tombs of Saints, the displacement of tens of thousands of people due to the ongoing violence and the catastrophic effect on the morale of the inhabitants of Timbuktu.

After Al Mahdi's judgment and sentence, the Trial Chamber issued a Reparations Order on 17 August 2017, the basis of which allowed the TVF to come up with an 'implementation plan' to help the victims. It defined the types of harm as:

1. Suffering to the people throughout Mali and the international community
2. Irreversible harm to the Protected Buildings
3. Consequential economic harm to the population of Timbuktu in general
4. Moral harm to the population of Timbuktu in general
5. Economic harm to some individuals directly in particular
6. Moral harm to some individuals directly in particular.

Individual and groups of victims were able to access forms both online and with the help of victim support groups in Timbuktu. After consultation, the TFV issued its preliminary report on how the 3.2-million-dollar reparation money should be spent. The report was cautious to avoid advocating the construction of any hurried memorials and instead to work within the principle of 'restorative agency', whereby the local community is empowered to decide for themselves whether and in what manner to memorialise the events of 2012. Money was put aside to provide professional mental health support for traumatised communities and to directly compensate those individuals most closely linked to the destroyed tombs.

The Drawers of Justice

The symbolism of the four drawers in the installation at the ICC – Genocide, Crimes against Humanity, War Crime and Crimes of Aggression – can be used to think about the way in which museum directors 'file' the letters they receive in relation to the return of the difficult collections in their care. What is airbrushed out of the display of colonial era collections in museums are the voices of the victims of the violence surrounding the looting and sacking of sites. Even the terms 'looting' and 'sacking' can be read at safe historical distance and do not have the same visceral effect as terms such as 'war crimes'. However, the emotional labour invested in a letter written by a community/descendent group or state in relation to their heritage should not be underestimated. This emotional labour is out of all proportion to the bureaucratic labour demanded of the museum director. What for the authors would be a letter that would fit in to one or more of the four ICC drawers/categories, could for the museum director simply be a letter put in to a drawer named 'legal'. This asymmetry is at the heart of the repatriation debate, where one party is invested body and soul and the other is invested in mind only. As the Sarr/Savoy report put it: 'Acquisitions of cultural heritage should be considered within a different category: that of transgressive acts, which no juridical, administrative, cultural, or economic apparatus would be capable of legitimizing' (2018: 8). The human suffering on display at the ICC may seem far removed from the world of museums yet many objects in museum were taken at a time of similar suffering. Furthermore, museums are increasingly seeing their role as one of advocacy for the recognition of human dignity.

The Proximity of Ethics

In April 2018 the Victoria and Albert Museum (V&A) opened its new Maqdala Exhibition, marking the 150th anniversary of the battle:

> The battle of Maqdala occurred on 13 April 1868 when British forces in Ethiopia attacked the troops of Emperor Tewodros, who was holding a British missionary and also an emissary. Seven hundred Ethiopian soldiers were killed, and the emperor committed suicide. British troops then looted the imperial possessions, including many Christian religious manuscripts and objects. Most of the loot was taken to the UK, with much of it eventually ending up in museums.[31]

In an interview with the *Art Newspaper*, the director of the V&A stated his commitment to returning the looted to treasure to Ethiopia, with the usual

---

[31] www.theartnewspaper.com/news/v-and-a-opens-dialogue-on-looted-ethiopian-treasures.

caveat: 'They would be sent to Ethiopia on long-term loan, so ownership would remain with the museum'.[32]

In an official press release, he described the importance of the exhibition:

> As custodians of a number of important Ethiopian objects taken from Maqdala by the British military 150 years ago, we have a responsibility to celebrate the beauty of their craftsmanship, reflect on their modern meaning, and shine a light on this collection's controversial history. By working closely with Ethiopian communities in London and the Ethiopian Embassy we are able to present this display with a new understanding of the collection's significance and share these objects with a new audience.[33]

At the same time, the V&A has been hosting a series of lectures, workshops and events as part of its 'Culture in Crisis' programme. Put in juxtaposition with the Maqdala case, the programme creates a number of contradictions. In its 'culture in crisis' mode, the V&A is a campaigning and outward looking institution, for example, in relation to Nazi looted art it is: 'exploring the development of ... provenance research ... to locate and remove Nazi-looted art from the collection'. The 'Culture in Crisis' programme is 'committed to protecting the world's cultural heritage and supporting communities that suffer cultural loss, whether through conflict, criminal acts or natural disaster'. Discussions about contemporary crimes against cultural heritage are hosted within the museum which funds the presence of global experts to consider reconstruction, digitisation and other protective measures.

Closer to home, together with other museums, the V&A has been working with victims of the Grenfell Tower disaster in London to help residents preserve and digitise the tributes left for the victims at the site.[34]

The paradox is therefore one of institutions that see themselves both as defenders of global cultural heritage, while housing collections that index the height of cultural destruction. On the official Maqdala blog,[35] the V&A states: 'These objects have been on display at the V&A for the past 146 years. They are stunning pieces with a complex history. Taken by the British Army during the 1868 Abyssinian Expedition, a number of objects from Maqdala are now held across several British cultural collections ...' The blog goes on to explain that museums have a responsibility to face the difficult histories of objects within their collections and that responsibility

---

[32] www.theartnewspaper.com/news/v-and-a-opens-dialogue-on-looted-ethiopian-treasures.

[33] www.telegraph.co.uk/news/2018/02/14/va-shine-light-british-looting-ethiopian-treasures/.

[34] www.thetimes.co.uk/article/top-museums-may-help-preserve-makeshift-tributes-to-grenfell-tower-victims-bnkdwd8ql.

[35] www.vam.ac.uk/blog/museum-life/maqdala-1868.

is in part fulfilled by exhibitions that attempt to tell the story from multiple viewpoints. For example, the exhibition is one of the few in the UK to describe the fate of people linked to the historical violence:

> Perhaps the most moving part of the Maqdala story is the fate of Tewodros's son, Prince Alemayehu. Terunesh's death left the prince an orphan at just seven years old. He was placed under the guardianship of a British army officer … (and)was brought to England, where the government assumed responsibility for his care and education. Maqdala 1868 includes a photograph of Speedy and Alemayehu taken by the famous photographer Julia Margaret Cameron, on a visit to Queen Victoria's Isle of Wight residence, Osborne House. Queen Victoria was particularly fond of Alemayehu, and was deeply saddened to learn that he had died in 1879 at the age of just nineteen. The inclusion of this photograph in the display juxtaposes Alemayehu with some of the other great treasures taken from Ethiopia, reminding us that not only material possessions were lost to the British forces.

That the voice of the victim included is one linked to Queen Victoria (and therefore documented in a museum ready way) is not surprising. The voices of other victims of colonial violence are much harder to recover and therefore usually silenced.

Guarantees of Non-recurrence

Part of the work of the TFV at the ICC is to require that states put in place measures to ensure a guarantee of non-recurrence: 'In response to massive human rights violations, states are obliged not only to prosecute the perpetrators, provide reparations to the victims and tell the truth about the violations but also to guarantee their non-recurrence' (Mayer-Rieckh, 2017: 416).

States can take measures such as desegregating education, putting infrastructural projects in place to better protect vulnerable communities and so on.

Could a museum with colonial era collections be envisaged along these lines? For example, museums could undertake to tell the truth about their collections, to provide reparations through return and to work towards guaranteeing non-recurrence by conceptually linking past cultural crimes to current ones and advocating on behalf of vulnerable communities. In the case of the V&A, they are already doing so, but perhaps inadvertently.

It is hard to see how museums can continue to describe themselves apolitical spaces, governed by aesthetics. Museums have always been and will remain political projects. Repatriation from museums is therefore always a political consideration, with the ethical pressure sometimes influencing the outcome but rarely as a point of departure.

However, as a mechanism for securing justice between parties, the restitution of objects plays a double role:

> If, following Aristotle, we regard the purpose of justice as the maintenance of an equilibrium of goods among members of society, the restitution interest presents twice as strong a claim to judicial intervention as the reliance interest, since if A not only causes B to lose one unit but appropriates that unit to himself, the resulting discrepancy between A and B is not one unit but two. (Fuller and Perdue in Virgo, 2006: 5).

Law and Ethics

At the moment, deliberations around the return of cultural objects from the UK take in to account multiple Conventions, Acts, laws and legal principles, to name but a few: the 1954 Hague Convention, the 1970 UNESCO Convention, the 1995 UNIDROIT Convention, the 2000 Human Tissue Act, the 2009 Holocaust Act, ICOM code of ethics, Museum Association ethics, Acts concerning the founding of museums (e.g. The British Museum Act 1963), the distinction in UK law between possession and ownership and so on.

It is therefore very difficult for claimants to be heard amidst this sea of legal complexity. It seems that a museum would fairly easily be able to hold on to objects should they want to. Conversely, museums find it very hard to deaccession (remove from their collection) objects – sometimes because the deaccessioning would contravene their founding statutes (in the case of national museums) and in other cases because such an eventuality was not foreseen by founders of museums, so trustees would have to try and fit within existing categories that allow for deaccessioning such as duplication, damage or objects not considered of use for future research.

It will probably soon be time for the UK Government to take the lead on dealing with colonial era contested collections. Following the path of reckoning over Nazi looted art, the ethical case currently being established in relation to colonial era collections will prepare the ground for legal conventions to follow. As can be seen by Macron's actions in France, countries across Europe are showing a new willingness to think about the ongoing consequences of colonialism as part of a reappraisal of the responsibility of democratic countries to act in the world. When Macron considers France's future relationship with sub-Saharan African countries, he can no longer do so while ignoring the past. Future relationships are constituted by past experiences where acts of contrition for past wrongs, both symbolic and literal, are essential for establishing new relational ethics.

Conclusion
Staging the Past in the Present

I presented an outline of this Element to Senegalese anthropology and archaeology PhD students at the University Cheikh Anta Diop in Dakar in February 2019. The diversity of their responses was a useful foil against any illusion of a straightforward link between cultural heritage, justice and dignity. Discussions covered the value of the past, the rupture with French colonial legacies, the consequence of Islamic faith on pre-Islamic cultural heritage, the politics of the use of language, both global and local, on and offline; and the validity of the concept of pan-African identity. Different students envisioned radically different heritage futures for themselves and their country (see figure 5).

Figure 5 Museum of Black Civilisations (Le Musée des Civilisations Noires), Dakar, Senegal. The museum opened on the 6th December 2018.
Credit: © Oumy Diaw

The heritage scene in Dakar at the beginning of 2019 was particularly interesting due to the recent opening of the new Museum of Black Civilizations. The museum had been funded by the Chinese Government and opened in time to meet a political deadline at the end of 2018. When I visited in February 2019 it was still half empty, with hastily assembled temporary exhibitions showcasing the museum's ambition. This ambition had been published as conference proceedings[36] and had identified some key elements central to the museum's identity:

> It will fulfil a mission that no global institution has ever fulfilled, that of preserving, documenting, strengthening, and showcasing the technological, scientific and cultural heritage connected to black civilisations. Next, the museum will position itself as a site of memory that will forever mark the culmination of a process – that of the affirmation of the recognition of the contribution of black civilisations to the heritage of humanity – where the starting point was, without doubt, the hosting in Dakar in 1966 of the World Festival of Black Arts.[37] (my translation)

Thus, the museum's stated ambition is to both take up the baton of the 1966 cultural achievement but also to inscribe a new history of black civilisations that corrects past silences: the role of Africa in the development of science and technology (see figure 6).

Figure 6 L'Arbre de L'humanité (the Tree of Humanity) by Edouard Duval Carrié in the main atrium of the Museum of Black Civilisations in Dakar.

---

[36] La Conférence internationale de préfiguration du Musée des Civilisations noires.

[37] Termes de référence Par Pr Hamady Bocoum, Directeur général du Musée des Civilisations noires et Dr El Hadji Malick Ndiaye, Conservateur du Musée Théodore Monod d'art africain/IFAN/CAD.

The museum's central atrium, which has a huge artistic rendition of a baobab tree (Edouard Duval Carrie's 2018 *L'arbre de l'humanité*), symbolises the waves of migration out of Africa. It is ringed by small interactive exhibitions about human evolution – one explanatory panel 'Africa: cradle of mankind' concludes: 'The lesson from history that should be taught in all schools is that from a strictly scientific point of view, everyone is originally from Africa on this planet (so*) Africans should feel at home everywhere*' (my translation and emphasis). Next, the museum has corridors exploring the African continent's contribution to science and technology. This space incorporates Egypt in its narrative. There are then rooms of photographs of black leaders – the men and women who have helped to shape the continent's intellectual and political landscape. One large room housed exceptional art including Benin Bronzes (that had previously been on display in United States), Nigerian terracottas, Dogon masks, a Malian Hunter's shirt hung with amulets, Chiwaras and many other iconic West African objects (see figure 7).

Figure 7 The sword and Coran of Ahmadou Tall (1836–1897). Taken by the French during the Battle of Segou (Prise de Ségou) in 1890. On loan from Le Havre Muséum d'histoire naturelle, France. The objects were originally donated to Le Havre in 1929 by Général Archinard.

A room dedicated to religion makes no reference to pre-Islamic or synchretic religion and instead celebrates the spread of Islam in Senegal and its charismatic male leaders. On loan from the French state is Ahmadou Tall's Qur'an and sword (taken during the 1890 siege of Ségou by French military officials and then given to the French state in 1929 by the Général Archinard). The continued presence of statues of French colonial officials in West Africa such as the two Louis – Archinard or Faidherbe – were a lively point of discussion for the Senegalese students mentioned above, many of whom wanted to see them removed from public spaces.

As is the case with all archives, the elements left out by the museum in this early incarnation of itself are as interesting as what is included. References to the trans-Atlantic slave trade were limited to artistic expression (one room housed many pieces from previous Dak'Art, Biennale of African Contemporary Art). Dakar is home to the Institutut Fondamentale de l'Afrique Noire (IFAN) museum whose collections have not been included in the museum. The IFAN museum holds a vast array of objects collected during the time of French colonialism from all parts of former French West Africa, a fact that many of the students were keen to point out – if the logic of international repatriation claims is followed, it would make sense to start thinking about regional repatriation to what are now independent nation states.

Another notable silence was Léopold Sédar Senghor, the first President of Senegal. He was a poet, writer and philosopher, a key figure in the *négritude* movement and architect of the 1966 Festival of Black Art referred to in the MCN's founding ambition document. While acknowledged as the intellectual forefather of the new museum in media interviews with museum officials, only one photograph of him (included on the wall with other notable black leaders) is on display. His former home in Dakar has been turned in to a private museum (bought by the Senegalese state to stop if from falling in to private hands). The house has been kept as it was when he lived there with his French wife, Colette Hubert, who became the First Lady of Senegal in 1960. The house is a cosmopolitan space, Senghor's bookcases overflowing with Greek philosophy, French literature, art history tomes and Russian novels. In one room, a beautiful Chagall painting is gently fading away, it has an inscription from the artist, a testimony to his friendship with Senghor.

Dakar, like everywhere else, is made up of layers upon layers of material fragments from the past, some curated and showcased as salient, others moth-balled and silenced as redundant. February 2019 was the time of general elections in Senegal and the manifestos of the presidential candidates represented the great diversity in the visions for heritage futures in the region. There was talk by one of the candidates of breaking the link with previous colonial oppressors through a change of currency (abandoning the currency that is pegged to the Euro). Other debates centred around the use of local languages in the educational curriculum or conversely, the importance of teaching all young people to speak English for them to be ready to fully participate in digital economies. Some of the candidates had a strong focus on Senegal's Islamic identity, others on its financial future and relationship with China. All the presidential candidates were aware of the demographic challenges of the region: a very young country, full of restless, ambitious and hyper-connected citizens who want answers to the challenges of poverty, low employment and lack of geographical mobility.[38]

Furthermore, the threat of regional insecurity is worrying many West African heritage practitioners. Whereas Senegal's museum infrastructure is growing rapidly, some countries, such as neighbouring Mali, are struggling to adequately care for their museums and prevent looting and damage to their archaeological heritage. The political unrest in Mali means that cultural heritage is vulnerable not only to the acts of radical Islamists as seen in Timbuktu, but also to the gradual decline of its heritage infrastructure due to lack of investment and training. Whereas the protection and promotion of cultural heritage in Mali was a priority for past governments (Joy, 2012), current events mean that the humanitarian crisis and ongoing violence in the region is testing the limits of its heritage professionals (cf. Hammer, 2017). Robust regional support networks would be a very valuable way to protect cultural heritage in the region. As Macron pledged during his 2017 speech in Ouagadougou:[39]

> This will also mean major work and a scientific and museum partnership, because – make no mistake – in many African countries it is sometimes African curators who have organized trafficking, and it is sometimes European curators or collectors who have saved those African artworks for Africa by protecting them from African traffickers. Our mutual history is sometimes more complex than we may instinctively think! The best tribute I can pay, not only to those artists but also to those Africans and Europeans who fought to safeguard those works, is to do everything possible to bring them back. It is also to do everything possible to ensure that there is security and that care is taken in Africa to protect those works. So these partnerships will also take every precaution to ensure that there are well-trained curators, academic commitments and government-to-government commitments to protect those works of art – in other words, your history, your heritage and, if you will allow me to say so, our heritage.

It can be inferred from many of the reactions to the Benin Dialogue group efforts to 'share' their collections that many in West Africa would not allow

---

[38] *Jeune Afrique*, Edition Afrique de L'Ouest, n#3032 17–23 Février 2019.

[39] www.elysee.fr/emmanuel-macron/2017/11/28/emmanuel-macrons-speech-at-the-university-of-ouagadougou.en.

Macron to say 'our heritage' as things stand today. Instead, the return of objects from European museums to Africa should be understood as a precondition to meaningful new relationships and not an end in itself. Macron identifying the complicity of African heritage professionals and the illegality and corruption rife in the international art market does not reduce the harm felt by those seeking the return of their cultural heritage. A proximity of blame does not seem like a very productive approach.

A Global Conversation: UNESCO's Role?

In 1977, the Senegalese Director-General of UNESCO, Amadou-Mahtar M'Bow, was asked to appeal to the British government to ask the British Museum to lend the Nigerian Government the mask of Queen Idia of Benin in time for the 1977 FESTAC Second World Black and African Festival of Arts and Culture festival in Lagos (discussed in 'Justice As Return'). He refused as he was worried that it would it would adversely affect broader conversations he was having about a global push to return cultural heritage to new the nations of Africa emerging from the shadows of colonialism. In 1978, he published a document entitled 'A Plea for the Restitution of an Irreplaceable Cultural Heritage to Those Who Created It'. It is a carefully worded and powerful document, one that over forty years later is still being ignored:

> One of the most noble incarnations of a people's genius is its cultural heritage, built up over the centuries ... The vicissitudes of history have nevertheless robbed many peoples of a priceless portion of this inheritance in which their enduring identity finds its embodiment ... The peoples who were victims of this plunder, sometimes for hundreds of years, have not only been despoiled of irreplaceable masterpieces but also robbed of a memory which would doubtless have helped them to greater self-knowledge and would certainly have enabled others to understand them better. Today, unbridled speculation, fanned by the prices prevailing in the art market, incites traffickers and plunderers to exploit local ignorance and take advantage of any connivance they find ... The men and women of these countries have the right to recover these cultural assets which are part of their being.
>
> They know, of course, that art is for the world and are aware of the fact that this art, which tells the story of their past and shows what they really are, does not speak to them alone. They are happy that men and women elsewhere can study and admire the work of their ancestors. They also realize that certain works of art have for too long played too intimate a part in the history of the country to which they were taken for the symbols linking them with that country to be denied, and for the roots they have put down to be severed.
>
> These men and women who have been deprived of their cultural heritage therefore ask for the return of at least the art treasures which best represent

their culture, which they feel are the most vital and whose absence causes them the greatest anguish.

This is a legitimate claim; and Unesco, whose Constitution makes it responsible for the preservation and protection of the universal heritage of works of art and monuments of historic or scientific interest, is actively encouraging all that needs to be done to meet it.

The return of cultural assets to their countries of origin nevertheless continues to pose particular problems which cannot be solved simply by negotiated agreements and spontaneous acts. It therefore seemed necessary to approach these problems for their own sake, examining both the principle underlying them and all their various aspects.

This is why, on behalf of the United Nations Educational, Scientific and Cultural Organization which has empowered me to launch this appeal,

I solemnly call upon the governments of the Organization's Member States to conclude bilateral agreements for the return of cultural property to the countries from which it has been taken; to promote long-term loans, deposits, sales and donations between institutions concerned in order to encourage a fairer international exchange of cultural property, and, if they have not already done so, to ratify and rigorously enforce the Convention giving them effective means to prevent illicit trading in artistic and archaeological objects.

I call on all those working for the information media – journalists of press and radio, producers and authors of television programmes and films – to arouse worldwide a mighty and intense movement of public opinion so that respect for works of art leads, wherever necessary, to their return to their homeland.

I call on cultural organizations and specialized associations in all continents to help formulate and promote a stricter code of ethics with regard to the acquisition and conservation of cultural property, and to contribute to the gradual revision of codes of professional practice in this connexion, on the lines of the initiative taken by the International Council of Museums.

I call on universities, libraries, public and private art galleries and museums that possess the most important collections, to share generously the objects in their keeping with the countries which created them and which sometimes no longer possess a single example. I also call on institutions possessing several similar objects or records to part with at least one and return it to its country of origin, so that the young will not grow up without ever having the chance to see, at close quarters, a work of art or a well-made item of handicraft fashioned by their ancestors.

I call on the authors of art books and on art critics to proclaim how much a work of art gains in beauty and truth for the uninitiated and for the scholar, when viewed in the natural and social setting in which it took shape.

I call on those responsible for preserving and restoring works of art to facilitate, by their advice and actions, the return of such works to the countries where they were created and to seek with imagination and perseverance for new ways of preserving and displaying them once they have been returned to their homeland.

I call on historians and educators to help others to understand the affliction a nation can suffer at the spoliation of the works it has created. The power of the fait accompli is a survival of barbaric times and a source of resentment and discord which prejudices the establishment of lasting peace and harmony between nations.

Finally, I appeal with special intensity and hope to artists themselves and to writers, poets and singers, asking them to testify that nations also need to be alive on an imaginative level.

Two thousand years ago, the Greek historian Polybius urged us to refrain from turning other nations' misfortunes into embellishments for our own countries. Today when all peoples are acknowledged to be equal in dignity, I am convinced that international solidarity can, on the contrary, contribute practically to the general happiness of mankind.

The return of a work of art or record to the country which created it enables a people to recover part of its memory and identity and proves that the long dialogue between civilizations which shapes the history of the world is still continuing in an atmosphere of mutual respect between nations.

Today, M'Bow's plea is still the starting point for UNESCO's work on restitution. What is striking about the plea is that it so reasonable. The logic of decolonisation should have led to the logic or return yet somehow it hasn't. The appeal to mutual respect and solidarity have been conveniently ignored. M'Bow is careful to ask for the return of those objects that are most important to people, he is not asking for the emptying of European museums but a gradual ethical, creative move, by ICOM and artists, academics and historians towards a rebalanced distribution of heritage.

Curators and Care

Many curators within museums in the UK agree strongly with M'Bow's words yet feel powerless to put them in to practice. Every now and then, curators can question institutional resistance through their work, even if inadvertently. For example, from May to August 2019, the British Museum included a display of the Manga artist Yukinobo's (2011) 'Professor Munakata's British Museum Adventure' in its blockbuster 'Manga' exhibition. 'The British Museum Adventure' tells the story of the Professor's investigations of the mysterious happenings at the British Museum following the disappearance of the Lewis Chessmen and the apparent demand for the repatriation of iconic artefacts from the museum's collections (including the Benin Bronzes). As the mystery unravels, a secret chamber under the museum is discovered containing long-laid plans to steal back the Rosetta Stone to avenge Napoleon. The story of European empire is interwoven with colonial acquired loot and British identity (with the Stonehenge megaliths taken as 'hostages' to force the British Museum's hand). The story is a lot of fun to read and a visually arresting portrait of the British Museum and its contents. It was published by the British Museum itself with the wry foreword by the then Director, Neil MacGregor: 'Perhaps we should not entirely approve of a storyline in which the landmark glass roof of the Great Court is smashed and a mysterious gang, with sinister airship, holds the British Museum to ransom to try and force repatriation of the Rosetta Stone' (2011: 6).

Yet the museum clearly does approve of it and is deliberately opening itself up to scrutiny. On one hand, Yukinobo's story is primarily a reassuring one: historically about European powers and dignity and about the ongoing care of the collections embodied by the young female curator who would give her life to preserve them. However, the fact that in the story the curator knows exactly where to turn when it becomes evident that repatriation is the key to solving the mystery is testimony to the diminishing space between the real world display of the Benin Bronzes and the hyper-real world of the manga British Museum.

From numerous conversations, despite a somewhat rigid reputation, it seems that the curators of contested collections are often those with the most open-minded views about the future care and destination of the objects in their care. They see their roles principally as custodians and therefore do not revert to the language of ownership and law as quickly as may be expected. Unlike the rigid, cold portrayal of the curator in Marvel Superhero film *Black Panther* who patronisingly dismisses questions from the film's antihero/hero about the mystery object she mistakenly thinks is from Benin, many curators have a lively interest in the critiques of their work, not just as a matter of diplomacy but from deep-rooted sense that questions of dignity and materiality matter, that their work matters. They therefore invite critique – in the form of conferences, artistic interventions, collaborations and so on, to shape the repatriation debate from within museums, sometimes in somewhat unexpected ways.

Resistance to return is much more likely found at the top, from museum directors and lawyers who would do anything to avoid having to set a career-ending precedent, or put their trustees in breach of Trust, or make a decision that proves to be an ill-judged reaction to present political pressures. A 'brave' director will inevitably emerge in the next few years, to be followed, if he/she doesn't fail, by others who will judge that there is more reputational risk for their institution if they do not engage with repatriation demands than if they do.

Dignity and Materiality

The numerous proverbs found throughout the world about the impossibility of ever truly 'going home' point to the existential dimension of the repatriation debate. If a return to the past is impossible, then repatriation of objects or reparations for victims is about forging new futures predicated on the ethical insights of the consequences of past events. Perhaps this approach seems naïve or simplistic, yet that could be seen as its strength, stripping away the layers of legal and scientific rationalism to expose a raw humanism, one that allows for gestures of generosity and repentance that are both symbolic and optimistic. For museums, there seems very little downside to adopting this new stance, inviting global audiences to think about objects' encounters with museums as a dynamic part of their journeys home, and if not ever truly 'home', then at least towards more ethical futures.

The demand for the return of cultural heritage is a demand for dignity. The link between human dignity and material culture is always present even if it does find different forms in different parts of the world at different times (including sometimes the conspicuous rejection of the material world in order to be more fully human).

When it comes to the demand for the return of human remains from museums, the proximity of current debates (for example the Human Tissue Act 2004 and Human Embryology and Fertility Act 2008) can be seen to inform how people feel about historic debates. Scandals, such as the Alder Hey Hospital scandal in Liverpool, which involved a pathologist ordering the removal of organs from dead infants without prior consent from parents, has awoken the public to the need to think about acceptable societal norms for the handling of human remains.[40]

The return of human remains from museums, whilst once contentious, has therefore now moved from the sphere of debate to one of broad agreement and museums all over Europe are actively participating in the process of return:

> In Europe alone, only the restitution of human remains seems to be progressively finding its way into the institutional consciousness: in 2002, France adopted a law authorizing the restitution of the mortal remains of Saartjie Baartman to South Africa ('Venus hottentote'); in 2002, several French museums restituted the remains of 21 Maori heads to New Zealand. In October 2017, the museums of Dresden gave back to Hawaii piles of bones and human remains that had been pillaged in the early 1900s.[41]

Perhaps the return of human remains, as compared to cultural objects, is the more clear-cut ethical case. It may also be that human remains are easier for museums to part with as bones and body parts are truly universal and not usually desirable for display. Nor can they be legally owned. Knowledge about them

---

[40] www.theguardian.com/uk/2005/jun/17/alderhey (accessed 30 September 2019).
[41] https://restitutionreport2018.com/sarr_savoy_en.pdf.

can be extracted and held in data banks (the next ethical battleground) and they do not have economic value akin to objects that exist in the shadow of the art market.

Museum objects are maybe held on to more tightly by museums as they resist ever being 'known' in a way that does not preclude future object/human relationships. Furthermore, curators consider themselves both custodians and connoisseurs and see their role as one of constantly reframing the objects in their collection to elucidate new meanings and new relationships.

The relationships we have with objects both define us and allow us to envisage different futures for ourselves, different ways in which we could exist in the world. The giving up of objects is therefore internalised by some museum professionals as a profound rupture, a closing down of future opportunities for educating, enchanting and simply showing people those objects they have been caring for so carefully for so long. For example, after the destruction of the Brazilian National Museum from fire in 2018, Beatriz Hörmanseder, a palaeontologist working at the Museum, had a tattoo of the building's façade etched on to her arm in order to cope with the trauma and loss following the fire. She has set up a project where other students and staff can do the same, thus creating a community visibly bound by loss.

However, the return of colonial era objects from European museum to their countries of creation is not a destructive act, a burning of scientific knowledge. It is instead an ethical and creative act of contrition, a precondition of new relationships that could allow Western museums to begin on their paths of decolonisation, dignity and justice.

Bibliography

Anderson, B. (1983) *Imagined Communities*. Verso.

Arendt, H (1963/2006) *Eichmann in Jerusalem: A Report on the Banality of Evil* Penguin.

Clark, K (2009) *Fictions of Justice: The International Criminal Court and the Challenge of Legal Pluralism in Sub-Saharan Africa* Cambridge University Press.

Coombes, A. (1997) *Reinventing Africa: Museums, Material Culture and Popular Imagination in Late Victorian and Edwardian England.* Yale University Press.

Cuno, J. ed. (2009) *Whose Culture? The Promise of Museums and the Debate over Antiquities.* Princeton University Press.

De L'Estoile, B. (2010) *Le Goût des Autres: de l'Exposition coloniale aux Arts premiers.* Flammarion.

Derrida, J. (1995) *Archive Fever: A Freudian Impression.* John Hopkins University Press.

Diagne, S. B. (2011) '*African Art as Philosophy: Senghor, Bergson and the Idea of Negritude*' Seagull Titles CHUP.

Gore, A. (2006) *An Inconvenient Truth: The Planetary Emergency of Global Warming and What We Can Do About it.* Bloomsbury.

Hammer, J. (2017) *The Bad-Ass Librarians of Timbuktu: And Their Race to Save the World's Most Precious Manuscripts.* Simon & Schuster.

Hobsbawn, E. & Ranger, T (1983) *The Invention of Tradition.* Cambridge University Press.

Jenkins, T. (2018) *Keeping Their Marbles: How the Treasures of the Past Ended Up in Museums – And Why They Should Stay There.* Oxford University Press.

Joy, C (2012) *The Politics of Heritage Management in Mali: from UNESCO to Djenne* Routledge.

Layiwola, P (2014) 'Making Meaning from a Fragmented Past: 1897 and the creative process' *Open Arts Journal*, Issue 3.

Lowenthal, D. (1985) *The Past is a Foreign Country.* Cambridge University Press.

MacGregor, N. (2012) *A History of the World in 100 Objects.* Penguin.

Mayer-Rieckh, A. (2017) 'Guarantees of Non-Recurrence: An Approximation'. *Human Rights Quarterly*, Volume 39, Number 2, May 2017, pp. 416–48.

Mbembe, A (2015) *Decolonizing Knowledge and the Question of the Archive* Africa is a Country ebook.

Morton, P. (2000) *Hybrid Modernities: Architecture and Representation at the 1931 Colonial Exposition.* MIT Press.

Ngom, F. (2018) *Le Silence du Totem.* Éditions L'Harmattan.

Nugent, M & Gaye Sculthorpe (2018) 'A Shield Loaded with History: Encounters, Objects and Exhibitions' *Australian Historical Studies*, 49:1, 28–43.

Ogunfolu, A. & Assim, M. (2012) 'Africa and the International Criminal Court'. *East Africa Journal of Peace and Human Rights*, Volume 18, Number 1, pp. 101–16.

Piketty, T. (2015) *The Economics of Inequality.* Harvard University Press.

Price, S (2007) *Paris Primitive: Jacques Chirac's Museum on the Quai Branly* University of Chicago Press.

Robertson, G. (2019) *Who Owns History? Elgin's Loot and the Case for Returning Plundered Treasure.* Penguin Random House.

Sarr, F (2016) *Afrotopia* University of Minessota Press.

Sarr, F. & Savoy, B. (2018) *Restituer le Patrimoine Africain.* Philippe Rey/ Seuil.

Thomas, D. (2013) *Africa and France: Postcolonial Cultures, Migration and Racism.* Indiana University Press.

Thomas, N (1991) *Entangled Objects: exchange, material culture and Colonialism in the Pacific* Harvard University Press.

Thomas, N (2018) 'A Case of Identity: The Artefacts of the 1770 Kamay (Botany Bay) Encounter' *Australian Historical Studies*, 49:1, 4–27.

Smith, Laurajane (2006) *Uses of Heritage.* Routledge.

Sørenson, M.-L. & Viejo-Rose, D. eds. (2015) *War and Cultural Heritage: Biographies of Place.* Cambridge University Press.

Vrdoljak, A. (2006) *International Law, Museums and the Return of Cultural Objects.* Cambridge University Press.

Yukinobu, H. (2011) *Professor Munakata's British Museum Adventure.* British Museum Press.

Virgo, G. (2006) *The Principles of the Law of Restitution.* Oxford University Press.

Acknowledgements

This is a short Element, yet it is the result of many conversations over the last few years with friends and colleagues around the world. The Element started with the generous intellectual input of colleagues at the Horniman Museum and Gardens in London.

I have many people to thank for their contributions including colleagues and students at Goldsmiths, University of London. At UNESCO, I am grateful for the insights of Lazare Eloundou. In Dakar, I received a warm welcome from Professor Ibrahima Thiaw and his students at the Université Cheikh Anta Diop. The Director of the Musée des Civilisations Noires, Dr Hamady Boucoum, and colleagues at the West African Research Centre provided invaluable advice.

At the International Criminal Court, I would like to thank Michelle Johnson for her help. Shona Ferguson generously shared her time and brought me in to conversation with Anthony Misquitta and Adrian Parkhouse whose legal expertise was invaluable. I would also like to thank Dr Jacques Schuhmacher at the Victoria and Albert Museum for our ongoing dialogue.

Some colleagues kindly read a draft of the Element, Dr Anita Herle and Professor Nicholas Thomas at the Museum of Archaeology and Anthropology in Cambridge, Professor Fallou Ngom at Boston University, Dr Ben Burt at the British Museum and Geoffrey Robertson QC of Doughty Street Chambers.

Finally, I would like to thank colleagues who had the idea for a series on Critical Cultural Heritage, in particular Professor Michael Rowlands, and those at Cambridge University Press who have brought the project together.

Cambridge Elements $^{\equiv}$

Critical Heritage Studies

Kristian Kristiansen
University of Gothenburg

Michael Rowlands
UCL

Francis Nyamnjoh
University of Cape Town

Astrid Swenson
Bath University

Shu-Li Wang
Academia Sinica

Ola Wetterberg
University of Gothenburg

About the Series

This series focuses on the recently established field of Critical Heritage Studies. Interdisciplinary in character, it brings together contributions from experts working in a range of fields, including cultural management, anthropology, archaeology, politics, and law. The series will include volumes that demonstrate the impact of contemporary theoretical discourses on heritage found throughout the world, raising awareness of the acute relevance of critically analysing and understanding the way heritage is used today to form new futures.

Cambridge Elements ☰

Critical Heritage Studies

Elements in the Series

Heritage Justice
Charlotte Joy

A full series listing is available at: www.cambridge.org/CHSE

Printed in the United States
By Bookmasters